THE STUDENT WORKBOOK
for
THE ART OF HELPING
EIGHTH EDITION

Robert R. Carkhuff

Debra Decker Anderson
AMERICAN INTERNATIONAL COLLEGE

Don Benoit
CARKHUFF INSTITUTE OF HUMAN TECHNOLOGY

John Linder
DELAWARE COUNTY COMMUNITY COLLEGE

Cheryl McLaughlin
NORTHERN VIRGINIA COMMUNITY COLLEGE

Copyright © 2000 by
Human Resource Development Press, Inc.
22 Amherst Road
Amherst, Massachusetts 01002

800-822-2801 (U.S. and Canada)
413-253-3488
413-253-3490 (fax)
www.hrdpress.com

For use with *The Art of Helping*, eighth edition
by Robert R. Carkhuff

ISBN 0-87525-575-9

Cover design by Eileen Klockars

TABLE OF CONTENTS

LIST OF EXERCISES

III. SUMMARY

1 Introduction

1. INTRODUCTION

This workbook is designed to help students and practitioners make the transition from reading about the helping skills in *The Art of Helping* to practicing these skills. The workbook does not replace a skilled professor or trainer, but serves as a supplement to your coursework or training. This series of exercises will give you an opportunity to practice using the helping skills with a wide variety of written helpee situations.

In addition to the use of this workbook and *The Art of Helping* text, a complete training program may include the following:

- Role playing with other trainees to practice using the skills

- Using the skills in a supervised practice experience

- Viewing *"The Art of Helping Video Series"*

- Practicing the skills using additional materials from *The Art of Helping Trainer's Guide*

- Using the skills to help yourself

- Using the skills in real-life helping situations

- Teaching the skills to helpees in real-life helping situations

This workbook has been used by students and practitioners in many professions; they include mental health therapists, rehabilitation and school counselors, teachers, nurses, nutritionists, social workers, business managers, personnel specialists, criminal justice workers, and others. It is useful for any individual who wishes to learn to relate effectively with others.

You will find that the overall organization of the workbook parallels the skills presented in *The Art of Helping*. Each skill, presented in *The Art of Helping,* has corresponding exercises in this workbook. These exercises are designed to help you *discriminate* levels of good and bad helping and *communicate* high levels of these same helping skills.

The range of problems, feelings, and types of people included in the workbook exercises represent the diversity you will likely encounter when you work with people. Practice with these varied helping situations will prepare you to handle a wide range of real-life helping situations. As you learn to lead yourself through the helpee phases of learning; *Exploration, Understanding* and *Action*, you will gain a clear mental image of the helping process, *Attending, Responding, Personalizing* and *Initiating*, one that will serve to guide you when helping others.

Students and practitioners find this workbook most helpful when they read the corresponding pages in *The Art of Helping* before they begin to complete the exercises. Preceding each series of exercises, the workbook gives you the page numbers of the corresponding section in *The Art of Helping*.

Now that you know where you are going with this workbook, you can begin learning the skills of helping. For some of you it will be an especially exciting journey because along the way you will meet many people and you will learn to help them. For others, it will sometimes feel frustrating because you will be eager to work with people, not books. Still others will feel hopeful because they will be learning important skills through a systematic program. After completing this workbook you will be more confident in your ability to work with "live people." This workbook is an opportunity for all of you to take the early, critical steps in mastering the "art of helping."

PRE-TEST

OVERVIEW

Before you use this workbook, find out what you currently know about the skills of helping. The following two pre-tests will give you the opportunity to evaluate both your ability to *communicate* helpfully and your ability to *discriminate* helpful responses.

A.   PRE-TEST: COMMUNICATING HELPING SKILLS

Instructions

Imagine that you have been talking with the following helpee for about 20 minutes. The helpee is a sixteen-year-old girl who is having problems with her parents. She says:

- Honestly! They treat me like I'm twelve, not sixteen. "Do this, be here, no you can't go...." Maybe I don't always act like an adult, but I think I've earned some responsibility. It's like they're afraid to let me out of their sight for fear of what I'll do. "We know best," they say. I can't wait 'til I can get away!

Now write down what you would say to this helpee. Write the exact words you would use if you were actually speaking to this girl.

you're anxious to leave, because your parents do not trust you enough to let you make you own decisions. You want to assert your inde- pendence but you feel that your parents are hindering you from doing so.

(Following training, you will have the skills to rate your response to this helpee. For now, you may ask an expert—your teacher or trainer—to rate your response.)

5

B.   PRE-TEST: DISCRIMINATING HELPING SKILLS

Introduction

Your training also involves learning to *discriminate* whether a response is effective or not. This pre-test will give you an idea of your current skill level at judging the effectiveness of a response.

Instructions

Imagine that a sixteen-year-old girl, who is having problems with her parents, has been talking with a helper for about 20 minutes. This is an excerpt of what she has been saying:

- Honestly! They treat me like I'm twelve, not sixteen. "Do this, be here, no you can't go...." Maybe I don't always act like an adult, but I think I've earned some responsibility. It's like they're afraid to let me out of their sight for fear of what I'll do. "We know best," they say. I can't wait 'til I can get away!

Listed below are several alternative responses that might have been made by someone trying to help this girl. Next to each response, write a number to indicate your rating of the effectiveness of that response. Use the following scale:

1.0	=	Very ineffective
2.0	=	Ineffective
3.0	=	Minimally effective
4.0	=	Very effective
5.0	=	Extremely effective

___4.0___ a. "You feel angry because your parents don't want to let you take responsibility for yourself."

___1.0___ b. "It *is* a pretty tough world out there, you know."

___2.0___ c. "You feel discouraged because you can't demonstrate that you're old enough to take responsibility for yourself and you want to prove yourself. A first step might be to list all the things you could do to prove responsibility; then, choose one to start with that your parents could accept."

___3.0___ d. "In other words, your parents seem to be too protective, too afraid to let you grow up."

___5.0___ e. "You're frustrated because you can't communicate to your parents that you have grown up and you want to clearly show them that you have."

(Once you have completed the discrimination pre-test you may turn to pages 214 and 215 of this workbook for answers to the discrimination pre-test and to record your ratings.)

GETTING READY FOR TRAINING

OVERVIEW

In completing your training experience, you will be playing the roles of both helper and helpee. The training experience will be much more fluid if you, when serving in the role of helpee, have a variety of topics which you can explore. These topics should be issues and concerns which are *real* to you for two reasons. First, you will eventually have to sustain exploration of a topic with others. This will require more than superficial exploration so you will need to identify issues that you will be willing to explore with others. Second, the feedback given to the helper will be more accurate and meaningful if your issues and feelings are real rather than hypothetical.

EXERCISE 1: EXPANDING TOPICS TO EXPLORE

Introduction

In preparation for playing the role of helpee during training, it is important to give some thought to the topics, problems, and concerns you want to explore. This exercise is designed to help you expand your list of available topics.

There are three basic resources that we, as humans, have in common:

- Physical: Body and energy level
- Emotional: Feelings and relationships with people
- Intellectual: Mind and all that is known

These basic resources are applied in the following areas:

- Living: The home setting
- Learning: The school or other learning environments
- Working: The job setting.

By creating a matrix with those resources and areas of functioning, you can begin to systematically expand your list of topics by exploring the issues within each category.

Example Matrix:

	PHYSICAL	EMOTIONAL	INTELLECTUAL
WORKING			Can't seem to learn the new procedure
LEARNING	Too tired to study at night	Can't get motivated to read books outside of school required assignments	Not living up to my potential
LIVING	Training for the first five-mile race	Problems with mother; getting along better with roommate	

Instructions

Using the matrix on the next page, begin to expand your list of topics. Within each cell, ask yourself, "What is happening in this part of my life that I am willing to explore with others?" The topics don't have to be major problems. They may be about something positive. They *do* have to be topics that will provide others, who will be practicing their helping skills, a chance to work with you.

You can refer back to this matrix throughout the course of your training and update your list as other possible topics for exploration come to mind.

TOPICS MATRIX

	PHYSICAL	EMOTIONAL	INTELLECUTAL
WORKING	1. Drains all of my energy 2. 3. 4.	1. It takes much longer to get accustomed to my duties 2. 3. 4.	1. 2. 3. 4.
LEARNING	1. I get too tired to study 2. 3. 4.	1. I don't have the motivation to study 2. I feel like I'm not doing well with my studies 3. 4.	1. Can't live up to my potential 2. Nothing seems to register in my mind 3. can't focus 4.
LIVING	1. I do not get enough sleep 2. 3. 4.	1. I'm overwhelmed with responsibilities 2. I get too distracted 3. 4.	1. 2. 3. 4.

EXERCISE 2: VIDEO EXERCISE—THE HELPING OVERVIEW

Introduction

The videotape *"The Helping Overview"* presents the helping model you will be learning. In the video Dr. Robert Carkhuff, two graduate students and a counseling professor undertake an active, informal and informative discussion of helping.

Instructions

View the video *"The Helping Overview."* Then diagram the helping model as you understand it. Use the space provided on this page for your drawing. Be sure to include the contributions of both the helper and the helpee. Compare your diagram with the information found on pages 1–50 of *The Art of Helping* text. Does your diagram accurately represent the helping model?

2

Helping
Skills

2. ATTENDING—INVOLVING THE HELPEE

OVERVIEW

The helper enables the helpee to become involved in a helping process through attending. Attending is defined as "paying attention to another person." Attending skills include: attending physically, observing, and listening.

EXERCISE 3: EXPLORING ATTENDING SKILLS

Introduction

The following exercise will help you become acquainted with your own attending skills.

Instructions

Stop! Don't move a muscle until you finish reading this!

Now, look at yourself. How are you sitting? What are you wearing? What does your facial expression look like?

Exercise

1. Describe yourself.

   I feel tired. Look distracted. I'm leaning on my right

2. From that description, what conclusions could you draw about yourself?

   That I'm not in the mood to talk to somebody or do anything

3. Are you sitting in a way that helps you to learn?

   NO

4. What could you change so that you would be better able to learn?

   Get some rest. Sit up straight. Stay focused

EXERCISE 4: VIDEO EXERCISE—ATTENDING SKILLS

Introduction

Physical attending, observing and listening are all necessary ingredients in the development of a constructive helper-helpee relationship.

Instructions

View the videotape *"Attending Skills."* This tape will overview the skills that helpers need to encourage helpee involvement. Then read pages 53–70 in *The Art of Helping* before completing the following seven exercises.

ATTENDING PERSONALLY

OVERVIEW

Attending includes preparing the helpee, preparing the helping context, preparing ourselves, and attending personally.

EXERCISE 5: DISCRIMINATING INVOLVING

Introduction

Helping will not occur unless the helpee becomes involved in the helping process. Therefore, prior to meeting with a helpee, you should inform the individual about the "who, what, when, where, how, and why (5WH)" of the proposed helping process. This is the first step in involving the person in the helping process.

The following example is a good illustration of involving because it tells *who* the appointment is with, *what* the purpose of the interview is, *when* and *where* it will be, *how* the person will get to meet Mr. Kennerly, and *why* the person should come to the interview. (5WH)

> "Hello, your appointment is with me, Mr. Kennerly, at 10 A.M. My office is Room 306 here at the clinic where you came on Friday. If you come to the receptionist in the main lobby, she will buzz me and I will come down to meet you. During this first meeting we'll be exploring the problems you expressed at intake. Our goal will be to list and specify a starting point so we can help you act to clear up these problems. You sound eager to start changing your life."

The following is a poor example of involving. It tells only *who* the appointment is with and *when*.

"Hello, I'm Ms. Schan. I've set your appointment for 3:00 Tuesday. I'll look forward to seeing you then."

Instructions

After reading the following example, identify the 5WH in each of the involving exercises.

Example

"I'd love to meet with you to see how you're doing! How about lunch on Saturday? I'll meet you at Nick's Cafe at 12:30. The two of us can have a relaxing lunch and talk about the progress you've made since we last saw each other."

WHO:	the two of us
WHAT:	meet for lunch
WHEN:	Saturday, 12:30
WHERE:	Nick's Cafe
WHY:	to talk about the progress she's made
HOW:	no specific directions given

Exercise

1. "Why don't you come by the house on Monday, Susie? We can talk then."

WHO:	_Susie_
WHAT:	_come by the house_
WHEN:	_monday_
WHERE:	_house_
WHY:	_to talk_
HOW:	_____

2. "The guard in your cell block says you've been complaining about your work assignment. I think it's a good assignment; it lets you work with machinery you're good at. Besides, I worked very hard to get that assignment for you. Anyway, I'm going to sign for you to come to my office and we'll talk about it. I'll explain it all to you then. I want you to understand my point of view. I don't know why you guys are never happy. I can't do much now, but come down. I'll see you."

WHO: _____

WHAT: _____work assignment_____

WHEN: _____

WHERE: _____office_____

WHY: _____to talk and explain_____

HOW: _____

3. "The lab called. They want to redo your tests. Hang around your room this afternoon so you'll be ready if they come by."

WHO: _____the lab_____

WHAT: _____lab tests_____

WHEN: _____in the afternoon_____

WHERE: _____your room_____

WHY: _____they want to redo tests_____

HOW: _____

16

EXERCISE 6: PRACTICING INVOLVING

Introduction

This exercise will give you a chance to practice involving others.

Instructions

After reading the sample statement presented below, write a statement that you might use to involve someone in your present or planned helping specialty (i.e., social work, medicine, criminal justice, education, etc.). Be sure to include the 5WH information.

Example

"Hello Jennifer, this is Mark Sampson from the Career Counseling Office. I'm calling to confirm our appointment for Friday at 10:30. My office is in the Bradley Building, Room 105. If you park in the back of the building and enter by the rear entrance, my office is the first door on the right. We'll take this first session to explore what you want to learn from our career counseling sessions."

Exercise

Your involving statement:

Hello Martha, this is Samantha Esteban from the Career Counseling Office. I'm calling to remind you of your appointment with me for Thursday at 2:30. My office is in Sheffield Hall, Room 234A. Just go to the receptionist at the lobby once you arrive. She will buzz me and I will come down to meet you. I am eager to help you learn to explore what type of career you want to go into.

17

EXERCISE 7: DISCRIMINATING CONTEXTUAL ATTENDING

Introduction

In any helping interaction, the furniture and environment should not create barriers or be distractions to the helping process.

Instructions

In this exercise, identify three environments where you often talk with friends and family. Briefly describe these contextual settings and identify their contextual strengths and deficits. An example is presented below.

Example

Environment:	Kitchen
Description:	Small kitchen with round table in front of a window.
Contextual strengths:	Warm, cheerful room
	Chairs can be moved closer or further away as appropriate
Contextual deficits:	Centerpiece, miscellaneous supplies on table create a barrier
	Family members use of kitchen can be distracting

Exercise

1. **Environment:** _Living Room_

   Description: _Large room with sofa, love seat, center table_

   Contextual strengths: _Roomy, comfortable space_
   Warm and inviting

   Contextual deficits: _Center table create a barrier_

2. **Environment:** _Kitchen_

   Description: _Small area with rectangular table in center_

   Contextual strengths: _Warm and comfortable room_
   Chairs can be moved closer or further
   away

   Contextual deficits: _Use of kitchen creates distractions_

3. **Environment:** _Bedroom_

   Description: _Large room with full size bed, armoire, TV_
   set

   Contextual strengths: _Allows for privacy and quiet conversa-_
   tions

   Contextual deficits: _Not the ideal room for attending_
   to someone you are not really close to

EXERCISE 8: DISCRIMINATING SELF-PREPARATION SKILLS

Introduction

Prior to meeting with a helpee you should; review what you know about him or her, identify your goal for the up-coming interaction, and eliminate or minimize any personal tension that you are experiencing.

Instructions

Identify the review, goal, and relaxation efforts in each of the three self-preparation stories. Read the following two examples before completing the exercise.

Example 1

Carol was having a long and very difficult day. She had two people who had called for emergency appointments. She was down to her last appointment of her day, which was one of the emergency appointments. With a deep breath she looked at her watch and then took a couple of minutes to read through the client's file. In particular, she read about their last session. She also tried to remember what the person had said on the phone and how the person had sounded. In her mind, she determined that she would help the person work through the emergency and then try to relate it to the goals already set for their time together. Finally, she sat back in her chair and closed her eyes. She took several long, deep breaths. Consciously she relaxed the muscles of her face, neck, shoulders, and the rest of her body. Once she was finished, she got up and went to the door to greet the waiting person.

REVIEW: Read through client's file

GOAL: Work through emergency, relate emergency to goals

RELAXATION: Deep breathing, relaxing muscles

Example 2

Chris was late getting into the office. He had overslept, exhausted from an active and fun weekend. His first appointment, Evelyn, was waiting. Glancing at his watch, he knew he was going to be behind schedule for the rest of the day.

"Good morning, Evelyn. How are you today?"

"I'm fine, Chris."

"Sorry, to keep you waiting. Let me get a cup of coffee and we'll get started."

Chris got himself a cup of coffee and then looked at his desk. There were two telephone messages and one cancellation. He smiled. It meant that he would catch up and even have a breathing space during the day. Still smiling, he went to the door and invited Evelyn into his office.

> **REVIEW:** None
>
> **GOAL:** None
>
> **RELAXATION:** Cup of coffee

Exercise

1. Joyce was regretting her appointment with Katherine. She really hadn't wanted to see her. On top of that, everything that could go wrong *had* gone wrong that day. The weather was hot and humid. The bus broke down on the way home so she had to walk the last two miles. Her air conditioner was broken and she didn't have time for a shower before Katherine would arrive. All she could think of was how tired and hungry she was and how badly she did not want to see Katherine. As Joyce was thinking this very thought, the doorbell rang.

   She opened the door to let Katherine in, greeting her with a distracted, tired, "Hi, come on in."

   > **REVIEW:** _None_
   >
   > **GOAL:** _None_
   >
   > **RELAXATION:** _None_

2. Marsha Miller walked down the hall to her office. Standing outside her door was one of her students, Mark. Mark was going to get a failing grade unless something drastic happened. As she got to the door, Mark said, "Hi, Dr. Miller, could I talk with you about class?"

"Sure, Mark. Just give me a minute, okay?"

Marsha went into her office and settled behind her desk. She took out her class records of Mark's class and reviewed his test scores and attendance. She noticed that he had done well on his two assigned papers, but not good enough to pass. With a sigh, she sat back and closed her eyes, letting her mind clear naturally. After a couple of minutes she went to the door and said, "Come on in, Mark."

REVIEW: _Look through class records_

GOAL: _NONE_

RELAXATION: _clear mind_

3. Charles wasn't looking forward to his lunch with Isabel. He knew that he would have to tell her some things about her behavior in the office that she wouldn't like hearing about. He sat back and thought of Isabel's behavior over the last couple of months: her increasing tardiness, the tired behavior, the short temper, and her avoidance of him and her co-workers. Yes, there was definitely something wrong. He decided that the best approach was to recommend that she see a counselor, but first he'd listen to what it was that had created these problems. That's all he'd do today, tell her what he had noticed and listen. Glancing at his watch, he saw he had a few minutes before twelve o'clock. Should he dictate the letter he needed to get done? No, he decided, and instead he sat back in his chair and let himself think of that ideal trout stream he found last fall. At noon, he got up and went to Isabel's office to meet her and walk to the restaurant.

REVIEW: _thought of past behavior_

GOAL: _tell Isabel what he had noticed and to listen_

RELAXATION: _sat back in chair and think of trout stream_

EXERCISE 9: PRACTICING SELF-PREPARATION

Introduction

This exercise will give you a chance to see how self-preparation applies to you and your relationships.

Instructions

Select someone you know who you really like. Write a brief description of your past two interactions with this person. Then write a goal for your next interaction, and a way you can relax before the actual interaction.

Exercise

Write out information about the other person, your goal, and plans for relaxation.

My friend Cheryl visited last summer after five years away from college. She visited for two days and we talked most of the time. We talked about our days in high school together, about our lives in college, and what we plan to do in the future. Our conversations were always lively and interesting and we can talk for hours and hours. Next time, I plan to meet and spend time with her much longer and to talk about serious and trivial things. I plan to go to a day spa to relax before meeting with her.

EXERCISE 10: ELIMINATING DISTRACTIONS

Introduction

It is important to remove any distractions from the helping environment so both helper and helpee can attend more fully.

Instructions

List 10 items or events that could be distracting during a helping interaction. Some examples are given below.

Example

Cold room temperature

Very loud background music

Exercise

1. _Very warm room temperature_
2. _phone ring_
3. _uncomfortable chairs_
4. _____
5. _____
6. _____
7. _____
8. _____
9. _____
10. _____

EXERCISE 11: DISCRIMINATING POSTURAL ATTENDING

Introduction

The helper's body should be positioned to communicate attention: squared, leaning forward, maintaining eye contact, and creating no distractions. A helper should also maintain an appropriate distance between himself or herself and the helpee.

Instructions

Observe the following people for three minutes while they are having a conversation with someone. List their postural attending deficits and assets in the space provided.

Example

Individual being observed: A father, talking with his son in the living room about possible colleges to attend

Postural Attending Deficits

(Leaning back in chair)

(Feet propped on coffee table)

(Not squared)

(Smoking)

_____

Postural Attending Assets

(Good eye contact)

(Appropriate distance between

     father and son)

_____

_____

Exercise

1.   Individual being observed: A family member, roommate, or friend

   Postural Attending Deficits   *Postural Attending Assets*

   lying down on couch   appropriate distance
   Not squared   Good eye contact
   _____   _____
   _____   _____
   _____   _____

2.   Individual being observed: A salesperson in a store making a sale

   Postural Attending Deficits   *Postural Attending Assets*

   Not squared   appropriate distance
   Not leaning forward   _____
   No eye contact   _____
   _____   _____
   _____   _____

3.   Individual being observed: An individual that you know talking with
                                    another person at school or work

   Postural Attending Deficits   *Postural Attending Assets*

   Leaning back in chair   Good eye contact
   Not squared   appropriate distance
   _____   _____
   _____   _____
   _____   _____

OBSERVING

OVERVIEW

Personal attending prepares us to observe. Observing is one of the greatest sources of learning about a helpee. The following exercises will help you practice your observation skills. See pages 71–78 in *The Art of Helping* for a detailed explanation of Observing.

EXERCISE 12: DISCRIMINATING DATA FROM INFERENCES

Introduction

It is important to look at concrete data first and then draw your conclusions from the data. Data consist of appearance and behaviors such as "a smile," "tears," and "clenched fists." In contrast, inferences are conclusions that we come to after we have seen the data. Examples include: "friendly person," "broken-hearted," and "steaming mad."

Instructions

Identify whether the following statements present data or inferences by checking the appropriate box.

Example

	DATA	INFERENCE
Open-minded		✓
Facial tick (spasmatic muscle contraction)	✓	

Exercise

	DATA	INFERENCE
1. Acts nervous	☑	☐
2. Ready to relate	☐	☑
3. Chewing lower lip, frowning, tapping foot	☑	☐
4. Looks excited	☐	☑
5. 5'8", broad shoulders, well-defined muscles	☑	☐
6. Overweight by 20 pounds, shirttail hanging out, patched jeans	☑	☐
7. Foxy chick	☐	☑
8. Looks like a con man, untrustworthy, sly	☐	☑
9. Eyes squint, looks sideways, slouches	☑	☐
10. Seems to be thinking about getting away	☐	☑
11. Guilty face if I ever saw one	☐	☑
12. Pale yelow skin, fast breath, hard pulse in neck	☑	☐
13. Slumping down in chair, round shoulders, leaning back, legs straight out	☑	☐
14. Approximately 40-years-old, wearing modern suit, tie matched for color, carrying briefcase, shoulders upright	☑	☐
15. Looks sad and obviously distressed about her life, a very unhappy person	☐	☑
16. Great body, sharp dresser	☑	☐
17. Good posture, looks attentive and interested with high energy level	☑	☐
18. Oh, how gross	☐	☑
19. Sitting upright, fully squared, direct eye contact, no nervous habits	☑	☐
20. Looks whacky as a fruitcake, a classic	☐	☑

EXERCISE 13:
DRAWING INFERENCES FROM OBSERVATIONS

Introduction

How group members look and act tell us a great deal about what their energy levels are and how they are feeling. Often we can make inferences about their levels of intellectual readiness and their degrees of congruence (agreement or consistency).

Instructions

Match these observations of appearance and behavior to the energy levels, feelings, levels of congruence, and intellectual readiness inferences that they might suggest. Place the letter(s) of the appropriate inferences next to the observations.

Example

	OBSERVATIONS	INFERENCES
a, c, e, g	Gesturing wildly, smiling	a. High energy
b, d, f	Eyes half open	b. Low energy
		c. Good-happy-positive feelings
		d. Sad-weak feelings
		e. High intellectual readiness
		f. Low intellectual readiness
		g. High congruence
		h. Low congruence

Exercise

	OBSERVATIONS		INFERENCES
1. _e_	Concentrating on tasks	a.	High energy
2. _b, d, f, h_	Head resting on arm, legs outstretched	b.	Low energy
3. _c, e, g_	Clean hair and clothes, fashionable, coordinated clothing	c.	Good-happy-positive feelings
4. _f, h_	Facing away from group leader	d.	Sad-weak feelings
5. _a, c, e, g_	Laughing and smiling	e.	High intellectual readiness
6. _e, g_	Good attending to group members	f.	Low intellectual readiness
7. _b, f, h_	Yawning	g.	High congruence
8. _b_	Very thin woman—5'6", 105 lbs.	h.	Low congruence
9. _b, f, h_	Slouched posture		
10. _b, f, h_	Dark circles underneath bloodshot eyes		

EXERCISE 14: OBSERVING EFFECTIVELY

Introduction

You have now had some practice discriminating data from inferences. The next exercise will help you organize and draw appropriate inferences. When practicing observing skills, it is helpful to organize your observations and inferences on a chart like the ones on the pages which follow. The charts will help you to check your observations of appearance and behavior for completeness and accuracy.

Instructions

Complete three observations of people using the following steps:

1. Select persons for observation as designated on the following pages.

2. Observe each person for at least three minutes.

3. Using the charts on the next few pages, record your observations of appearance and behavior.

4. Based on these observations, circle your inferences about each person's energy level.

5. Circle your inferences about each person's feelings.

6. Circle your inferences about each person's level of congruence.

Example

Situation: Observation of a young man standing on a street corner.

APPEARANCE	BEHAVIOR	INFERENCE
Posture: Standing slouched, leaning against a building	**Body Movements:** Slow hand and arm movements while smoking a cigarette	**Energy Level:** High – Medium – (Low)
Facial Expressions: loosly hanging mouth, eyes downcast		**Feelings:** Up – Mixed – (Down)
Grooming: torn t-shirt, dirty jeans, dirty sneakers with holes, shaggy haircut, hair hanging in eyes		
Body Build: about 6 foot tall and 150 pounds, thin		**Congruence:** (High) – Medium – Low
Sex: male		
Age: early 20's		
Race: white		

Exercise

1. Situation: Observe a person you know well in school or at work.

APPEARANCE	BEHAVIOR	INFERENCE
Posture: slouched	**Body Movements:** sluggish movements	**Energy Level:** High – Medium – (Low)
Facial Expressions: frowning eyes drooping		
Grooming: well dressed, hair neat		**Feelings:** Up – Mixed – (Down)
Body Build: 5'3", 130 lbs small frame		
Sex: F		**Congruence:** High – Medium – (Low)
Age: 40's		
Race: White		

2. Situation: Observe a person you know slightly in school or at work.

APPEARANCE	BEHAVIOR	INFERENCE
Posture: standing up straight	**Body Movements:** energetic fast movements	**Energy Level:** (High) – Medium – Low
Facial Expressions: smiling, laughing		
Grooming: well dressed, neat hair		**Feelings:** (Up) – Mixed – Down
Body Build: 5'3" 160 lbs medium frame		
Sex: F		**Congruence:** (High) – Medium – Low
Age: late 30's		
Race: White		

3. Situation: Observe a person you do not know.

APPEARANCE	BEHAVIOR	INFERENCE
Posture: Leaning back on chair **Facial Expressions:** frowning, eyes looking sideways **Grooming:** clean hair and clothes well groomed **Body Build:** 5'8" medium frame 150 lbs. **Sex:** F **Age:** mid 20's **Race:** White	**Body Movements:** constant hand gestures while talking on phone and smoking	**Energy Level:** High – (Medium) – Low **Feelings:** Up – (Mixed) – Down **Congruence:** (High) – Medium – Low

LISTENING

OVERVIEW

An effective listener can recall content specifics, identify a theme and identify the feelings expressed by a speaker. This means recalling who was spoken about, what the general topic was, when and where it happened, and why and how it occurred. Before doing the following exercises, review pages 79–86 in *The Art of Helping*.

EXERCISE 15: PRACTICING LISTENING SKILLS

Introduction

In this exercise, you will practice listening and identifying the who, what, when, where, why, and how (5WH) of a statement.

Instructions

Read the statements in this exercise aloud, listening for the who, what, when, where, why, and how (5WH) information. Cover the statement with a sheet of paper and record your answer for each interrogative. Finally, re-read the statement and identify what you heard correctly or incorrectly, and what you missed.

Example

"I just talked with my sister in Idaho. She's really upset—cried the whole time we talked. She got pregnant three months ago and yesterday she miscarried. She really wanted this baby."

WHO:	Sister
WHAT:	Upset about miscarriage
WHEN:	Yesterday
WHERE:	Idaho
WHY:	Really wanted the baby
HOW:	Not applicable

Exercise

1. "What a high! We had a little wine, smoked some grass, and had a really good time. Now you're telling me I should quit! No way!"

   WHO: _____

   WHAT: _____

   WHEN: _____

   WHERE: _____

   WHY: _____

   HOW: _____

2. "I've been in and out of school for the past five years, you know. I've worked odd jobs here and there. None of the things I've tried use much of me. I keep thinking I should finish school and find something better, but damned if I know what that is."

   WHO: _____

   WHAT: _____

   WHEN: _____

   WHERE: _____

   WHY: _____

   HOW: _____

3. "I'm scared! The tooth hurts so much, but so does the dental work. I don't know which is worse. My friend had a root canal done and it caused all kinds of complications—put him in the hospital for a week. How do I know that won't happen to me?"

   WHO: _____

   WHAT: _____

   WHEN: _____

   WHERE: _____

   WHY: _____

   HOW: _____

4. "These ADC payments just don't last. I scrimp and save and still my kids wear rotten clothes, have no food—they're always hungry. I don't know how I'm expected to make it. I feel like I'm being punished and I'm only trying to raise my kids. Christ! They'd do better as foster children than I can do for them."

WHO: _____

WHAT: _____

WHEN: _____

WHERE: _____

WHY: _____

HOW: _____

5. "The guard on that late night shift has it in for me. I ain't done nothin'—just trying to do my time—peaceful as a kitten. He keeps naggin' me, though...I'm gonna kill the bastard!"

WHO: _____

WHAT: _____

WHEN: _____

WHERE: _____

WHY: _____

HOW: _____

EXERCISE 16: PRACTICING ATTENDING SKILLS

Introduction

This exercise will help you apply all of your attending skills in a familiar context.

Instructions

Watch a TV show. Attend physically while watching the show. After the first 10-minute segment of the show, complete the following exercise.

Exercise

1. Check your own physical attending.

    - *Attending contextually:* Was the room arranged so that you had an excellent view of the TV set? Was the room arranged for your comfort?

        ☑ Yes   ☐ No

        If no, what was wrong? _____

        _____

        _____

    - *Attending personally:* Where you hungry or tired while watching?

        ☐ Yes   ☑ No

        If yes, what was wrong? _____

        _____

2. Identify the two characters you liked best.

    Character 1 — _____

    Character 2 — _____

    For each character, complete the following observing and listening charts:

Character #1

- Observing the character:

APPEARANCE	BEHAVIOR	INFERENCE
Posture:	**Body Movements:**	**Energy Level:** High – Medium – Low
Facial Expressions:		**Feelings:** Up – Mixed – Down
Grooming:		
Body Build:		**Congruence:** High – Medium – Low
Sex:		
Age:		
Race:		

- Listening to the character:

Who did the character talk with? _____

_____

What did they talk about? _____

_____

_____

When did this occur? _____

Where did this occur? _____

Why did they talk to each other? _____

_____

How (process) or how well (quality) did the conversation go? _____

_____

_____

Character #2

- Observing the character:

APPEARANCE	BEHAVIOR	INFERENCE
Posture:	*Body Movements:*	*Energy Level:* High – Medium – Low
Facial Expressions:		*Feelings:* Up – Mixed – Down
Grooming:		
Body Build:		*Congruence:* High – Medium – Low
Sex:		
Age:		
Race:		

- Listening to the character:

  Who did the character talk about? _____

  _____

  What did they talk about? _____

  _____

  _____

  When did this occur? _____

  Where did this occur? _____

  Why did they talk to each other? _____

  _____

  How (process) or how well (quality) did the conversation go? _____

  _____

  _____

3. RESPONDING—FACILITATING HELPEE EXPLORING

OVERVIEW

In the previous section you learned how to involve the helpee by using attending, observing, and listening skills. Now you will learn to help another person to fully explore himself or herself. In this section, you will learn to *respond* or verbally communicate your understanding of the helpee's experiences. You will communicate your understanding by responding at an interchangeable level to the content, feelings, and meanings expressed by the helpee.

The exercises contained in this section will first teach you "Responding to Content." Next, you will learn "Responding to Feeling." Finally, you will combine them in "Responding to Meaning." Refer to pages 95–130 in *The Art of Helping* for information about responding.

EXERCISE 17: EXPLORING RESPONDING SKILLS

Introduction

This exercise will help you become acquainted with the importance of responding. When people respond, they communicate an openness to another person's point of view.

Instructions

Take a moment to think about the importance of responding to another person's experience.

Exercise

Think of the last time you had an argument with a friend (or your mother/father/ employer). Think about what the argument was about, what you did or said, and what the other person did or said. Would you have been more willing to explore both sides if he or she had communicated an understanding of your point of view? Why?

_____

_____

_____

_____

RESPONDING TO CONTENT

OVERVIEW

A good response to content should paraphrase what was said as concisely as possible and without parroting all the details. To make sure you understand the skill, review pages 100–103 in *The Art of Helping*.

EXERCISE 18: DISCRIMINATING SPECIFIC RESPONSES

Introduction

Responses to content should be specific, not vague. Vague responses do not facilitate exploration. Specific responses help clarify the helpee's experience which facilitates exploration.

Instructions

Identify whether the following responses are specific or vague.

Example

Student: "I'm so tired, I don't know what to do. I try to keep up with everything: work, home, classes. But each day seems so long, by noon I'm already too tired to cope."

a.   You're saying you're tired.

☐   Specific   ☑   Vague

b.   You're saying there's so much to do that you don't have the energy to do it all.

☑   Specific   ☐   Vague

Exercise

Mother: "My children are starting to get out of hand. They've gotten so they don't listen to me or my husband unless we threaten them. And who wants to always have to threaten their kids?"

1. You're saying your kids are too wild.

   ☐ Specific   ☐ Vague

2. You're saying your children don't behave unless you or your husband threaten them.

   ☐ Specific   ☐ Vague

3. You're saying you don't want to have to threaten your kids to get them to be obedient.

   ☐ Specific   ☐ Vague

4. In other words, your children don't obey until you threaten them in some way.

   ☐ Specific   ☐ Vague

5. In other words, you don't want to have to do this.

   ☐ Specific   ☐ Vague

6. You're saying you don't like this behavior.

   ☐ Specific   ☐ Vague

EXERCISE 19: DISCRIMINATING PARAPHRASING vs. PARROTING

Introduction

Responses to content should paraphrase the original expression and not "parrot." By using different words to express the same content, paraphrasing adds a fresh perspective and facilitates exploration.

Instructions

Identify whether the following responses "parrot" or paraphrase the original expression.

Example

Boyfriend: "Well, she's finally talking to me again. It's not the same but at least we're talking. I still feel awful about the things she thinks I said about her. I would never say or do anything to hurt her. I think too much of her."

a. You're saying she's finally talking to you even though it's not the same. You feel awful about what she thinks you said because you would never do anything to hurt her.

[✓] Parrot   [ ] Paraphrase

b. You're saying that you are slowly straightening out the misunderstanding and you're talking to each other again.

[ ] Parrot   [✓] Paraphrase

44

Exercise

1. "I'm stuck. My boss refused to let me do the new project my way. I didn't check until I'd done 40 hours of work and now I've got to redo the whole thing by Monday morning."

   a. You're saying that you're stuck because your boss refused to let you do the project your way and now you've got to redo the whole thing by Monday morning.

   ☐ Parrot   ☐ Paraphrase

   b. You're saying that you have to invest all that effort again.

   ☐ Parrot   ☐ Paraphrase

   c. You're saying that you didn't check in time and now you're in a tight spot.

   ☐ Parrot   ☐ Paraphrase

2. "Thanks for all the help you've given me this semester. I was pretty mixed up when I got here, but now I really feel I've got it together. I'm passing all my courses for the first time."

   a. You're saying you're succeeding academically and I made a difference.

   ☐ Parrot   ☐ Paraphrase

   b. You're saying that you appreciate my help this semester. You've gotten it together and you are passing all your courses.

   ☐ Parrot   ☐ Paraphrase

   c. You're saying you feel pleased with the effect my assistance has made on your schoolwork.

   ☐ Parrot   ☐ Paraphrase

EXERCISE 20: DISCRIMINATING BRIEF RESPONSES

Introduction

Responses to content should be brief without losing specificity.

Instructions

Identify whether the responses are <u>too long</u> or <u>brief and specific</u>.

Example

Employee: "Damn, I blew it again! I just don't seem to be able to think before I open my big mouth. This job was going so smoothly until I got mad and told off my supervisor."

1. You're saying you messed up by exploding at your supervisor.

    ☐ Too Long   ☑ Brief and Specific

2. You're saying that everything was going well but you went and messed it up by mouthing off just like you always do and now, since you went and yelled at the supervisor, it isn't so good at work and you sound like you could have lost your job.

    ☑ Too Long   ☐ Brief and Specific

Exercise

Alcoholic: "I just can't give up my drinking. I've tried and tried and I can't. I get some money in my pocket and I have good intentions but I just buy more beer and wine."

1. You're saying you can't quit drinking even though you've tried. You always spend your money on booze.

   ☐ Too Long   ☐ Brief and Specific

2. In other words, you always buy booze even when you're trying to quit.

   ☐ Too Long   ☐ Brief and Specific

3. You're saying you can't give up the beer and wine. Even though you try not to buy any, it seems like if you get money you go to the store and that's what you spend your money on. Even having good intentions doesn't make a difference with you.

   ☐ Too Long   ☐ Brief and Specific

4. In other words, you can't quit drinking. You try and try and yet it just seems that when you get money that's how you spend it. Even when you have good intentions and you're trying to quit, you buy booze with your money.

   ☐ Too Long   ☐ Brief and Specific

5. You're saying giving up drinking isn't easy for you no matter how good your intentions.

   ☐ Too Long   ☐ Brief and Specific

EXERCISE 21: DISCRIMINATING NONJUDGMENTAL RESPONSES

Introduction

Responses to content should be nonjudgmental. A judgmental response adds a new conclusion, interprets the other person's behavior as good or bad, or distorts what the person actually said. This exercise will help you to identify responses that are judgmental.

Instructions

Identify whether the following helper's responses are judgmental or nonjudgmental.

Example

Grandparent: "Oh leave me alone. I know what I'm supposed to do but I'll be damned if I'll sit around and let someone else tell me what to do."

1. You're saying you know better than they do and that gives you the right to ignore them.

   ☑ Judgmental   ☐ Nonjudgmental

2. You're saying you don't want to be pushed around.

   ☐ Judgmental   ☑ Nonjudgmental

Exercise

Student: "That damn teacher! She doesn't even look at my work. Her comments are so ridiculous. And she's picky about such little things: misspelled words and poor handwriting. Those have nothing to do with what I know about a subject."

1. You're saying the teacher judges your work on the wrong qualities and it's unjust.

   ☐ Judgmental   ☐ Nonjudgmental

2. You're saying you're too dumb to do high quality written work.

   ☐ Judgmental   ☐ Nonjudgmental

3. In other words, you think the teacher is pretty unfair to you. You think she should take the broad view instead of being so picky.

   ☐ Judgmental   ☐ Nonjudgmental

4. You're saying it's easier to blame the teacher than to take responsibility yourself for details.

   ☐ Judgmental   ☐ Nonjudgmental

EXERCISE 22: DISCRIMINATING GOOD CONTENT RESPONSES

Introduction

This exercise will help you identify effective and ineffective responses so that you can evaluate and improve your own future responses.

Instructions

Rate each response and state the reason for your rating.

Example

Student: "I don't know...school just isn't living up to my expectations. I thought that when I got here life would be different than before—that classes would be exciting, that there'd be a lot of parties to go to, that I'd be doing loads of great things. But it seems that my classes are only reviewing, and me and a bunch of other guys just end up sitting around and doing nothing much. School is no better than staying home and working for my father."

	GOOD	POOR
1. It's too bad you feel that way. There really is a lot to do—if you go out and find it.	☐	✓

    Reason: *Does not indicate the helper really heard the speaker; it contradicts the helpee's statement; judgmental*

	GOOD	POOR
2. You're saying that this is no better than home, that you expected new school work and lots of parties but you just end up sitting around with the guys and not doing anything much.	☐	✓

    Reason: *Parrots back most of the details without summarizing the essential point; it is not brief enough*

	GOOD	POOR
3. You're saying that school hasn't given you what you were looking for—something new and exciting.	✓	☐

    Reason: *Sums up what the speaker said in brief, paraphrased response*

Exercise

Ball Player: "That coach! He spent all week telling me 'This game I'll play ya,' and then at last night's game, he ignored me. Not once did I play."

	GOOD	POOR

1. You're saying, "That coach! He spends all week telling you 'this game, I'll play ya,' and then at last night's game he ignored you." You didn't play once. ☐ GOOD / ☑ POOR

   Reason: _parrots back what the speaker said_

2. You're saying the coach was rotten. ☐ GOOD / ☑ POOR

   Reason: _judgmental, too short, does not demonstrate understanding_

3. You're saying the coach set you up so you expected to play and then he didn't follow through on his word. ☑ GOOD / ☐ POOR

   Reason: _sums up what speaker said, paraphrased response_

4. You're saying the coach wasn't too cool. He told you, "You'll play," and you were all ready for it to happen. Yet when last night's game came along, it turned out that he had really misled you. I mean, here he'd told you you would play and then he left you sitting on the bench the whole game. You never got any playing time from that coach. ☐ GOOD / ☑ POOR

   Reason: _Too long, parrots back some of what the speaker said_

5. In other words, the coach let you down badly after encouraging you and building up your expectations. ☑ GOOD / ☐ POOR

   Reason: _sums up what speaker said in brief._

Introduction

You have now had some practice in discriminating helpful responses to content. You are ready to begin developing your own responses. Writing responses will make it easier for you to make verbal responses later.

Instructions

Review the elements of a good response to content, then write your best response to the content expressed in each of the following statements.

Example

Young Man: "I've been thinking about joining the ROTC. My friends are really giving me a bad time about it. But I need some sort of job and jobs are hard to find around here. I'm not sure what to do."

You're saying <u>that you really need to find a job but you're not sure if ROTC is the answer.</u>

Exercise

1. Student: "I think I've been railroaded. Some members of the Student Government asked me to head a committee for Parents' Day. They said it wouldn't be too much of a job but nobody seemed to be able to give me any details. Then they told me they'd send me some materials later. So now I've heard some rumors about the plans but I still don't know anything for sure."

You're saying _that the SG offered you a job but did not give you any information about it which made you feel that they have been unfair to you_

2. Teenager: "I didn't do anything. I was just standing here and some guy goes running by me and then I heard you yell at me to stop. So I stopped."

You're saying _you are innocent and that you stopped because you were told to._

3. Woman: "Sometimes it seems like nothing I do ever turns out right."

You're saying _that there are times when anything you choose to do seem insignificant and wrong_

4. Employee: "This guy is impossible to work with. He stands over my shoulder and constantly tells me what I'm doing right, what I'm doing wrong, how to adjust this, what to change there!"

You're saying _that this guy makes it difficult for you to work with him because of his constant criticism_

5. Student: "The teacher is always on my friend's back; nothing Tommy ever does is right, and every time Tommy moves wrong, ZAP! he gets it."

You're saying _that the teacher is always very critical and disapproving of Tommy_

6. Businesswoman: "My career just doesn't seem to be going anywhere. The choices I've made in the past have all been dead ends. There are never any future opportunities in the jobs I accept."

You're saying _that the career choices you've made has given you no room for advancement and growth._

7. Homemaker: "I've finally found a group of people who really offer what I want in friendships. They are mature, reliable, fun-loving, decent, and have some backbone—a sense of who they are without being weak or somber. They make me feel good."

You're saying _that you have finally found people who possess the qualities you look for in friends and that these friendships make you happy._

8. Ex-convict: "I've been looking hard for work but they don't give you a fair break once they know you've got that prison record. They judge the record, not the man. They leave no room for people who have changed."

You're saying _that finding a job has been difficult because your prison record has been used by people as a basis to make unfair judgements on you._

9. Patient: "No one has told me a thing. I feel like I'm just a disease laying here—not a person! No one treats me like they even see me."

You're saying _that people treat you as if you are someone insignificant_

10. Father: "I need help. I got laid off two months ago and we didn't have much savings. Just living these past two months ate up our money pretty quick. I can't even buy my kids new school supplies this year."

You're saying _that your recent unemployment has dried you up financially and you need some sort of assistance._

RESPONDING TO FEELING

OVERVIEW

When formulating a verbal response to the feelings of another person, it is useful to have a large vocabulary of feeling words available to you. From this feeling word vocabulary you will select words that are *appropriate to the person's frame of reference* including selection of feeling words that are accurate in *feeling category* and accurate in *intensity*.

Before completing the exercises in this section, review pages 104–116 in *The Art of Helping*.

EXERCISE 24: DISCRIMINATING ACCURATE FEELING RESPONSES

Introduction

Knowing if a feeling word is accurate or inaccurate prepares you to make better responses to feelings.

Some reasons that a response to feeling may not be accurate are:

- The category is wrong

- The intensity is off

- The response comes from the helper's frame of reference, not the frame of reference of the other person

- It does not use a feeling word

Instructions

In this exercise rate the accuracy of the feeling word in each response. After rating each response, state your reason for your rating. Use the following ratings:

        (+)   If the response is accurate

        (-)   If it is not accurate

Example

Roommate: "I just don't understand it! I walked into my room this afternoon and my roommate totally ignored me! I asker her what was wrong; she looked at me and said, '*You* should know,' then left. I felt about an inch tall. And, no one else will tell me anything, either. What am I supposed to do if no one will let me in on it?"

1. Response: You feel that they're keeping something from you.
   Rating: ☐ (+)   ✓ (-)
   Reason: <u>No feeling word</u>

2. Response: You feel furious!
   Rating: ✓ (+)   ☐ (-)
   Reason: <u>Accurate category and intensity</u>

3. Response: You feel petrified.
   Rating: ☐ (+)   ✓ (-)
   Reason: <u>Inaccurate category and intensity</u>

Exercise

1. Wife: "I don't know what's wrong between my husband and me. When we got married we were so close, and now there is a void between us. We just don't communicate anymore."

   a. Response: You feel empty.
      Rating: ☐ (+)   ☐ (-)
      Reason: _____

   b. Response: You feel devastated.
      Rating: ☐ (+)   ☐ (-)
      Reason: _____

   c. Response: You feel relieved.
      Rating: ☐ (+)   ☐ (-)
      Reason: _____

2. Dropout: "I missed the appointment. The damn bus was late and then it was farther from the bus stop than I thought. Now I have to wait another three months to take the G.E.D. I really wanted to get that degree now."

    a.   Response: You feel furious.

            Rating: ☐ (+)   ☐ (-)

            Reason: _____

    b.   Response: You feel resentful.

            Rating: ☐ (+)   ☐ (-)

            Reason: _____

    c.   Response: You feel disappointed in yourself.

            Rating: ☐ (+)   ☐ (-)

            Reason: _____

3. Teacher: "The teacher's aide I got this year is a real 'winner.' She acts like she's 14—and that's being kind. I don't know how I'm gonna make it through the year with her."

    a.   Response: You feel discouraged.

            Rating: ☐ (+)   ☐ (-)

            Reason: _____

    b.   Response: You feel irritated.

             Rating: ☐ (+)   ☐ (-)

            Reason: _____

    c.   Response: You feel devastated.

            Rating: ☐ (+)   ☐ (-)

            Reason: _____

EXERCISE 25: CHOOSING ACCURATE FEELING WORDS

Introduction

You will often find that several feeling words accurately capture the person's experience. You will be more likely to identify the most accurate feeling if you first explore their many possible feelings.

Instructions

Circle the feeling words that accurately identify (category and intensity) the feelings of the speaker.

Example

Young man: "I finally found some people I can really get along with. There's no pretentiousness about them at all. They're real and they understand me. I can be myself with them."

How would I feel if I were this person?

(a.)	happy	d.	confused	g.	skeptical
b.	worried	e.	let down	(h.)	excited
(c.)	delighted	(f.)	good	i.	gratified

Exercise

1. Teenage Employee: "I'm sick and tired of being the 'go-for' in that office. I've been working there for six months now and I think that I should have earned some responsibility."

How would I feel if I were this person?

(a.) fed up		d. furious		g. surprised
b. happy		e. insecure		h. confused
c. ignored		f. amused		(i.) used

58

2. Sibling: "I wish I knew what I could do. My sister and my parents are fighting again. *Nothing* she ever does is right in their eyes—like she's damned if she does and damned if she doesn't. Yet, they do have a point. Sometimes she doesn't show any sense."

How would I feel if I were this person?

a.	intrigued	(d.)	frustrated	g.	lucky
(b.)	troubled	(e.)	sad	(h.)	torn
c.	excited	f.	tired	(i.)	upset

3. College Student: "I finally got up enough nerve to talk to 'Hurricane Hilda' about my paper. I was honest about the trouble I've been having. I did what we worked out, you know, I responded to her. And it worked! I'm all set with my paper and I discovered she's human too."

How would I feel if I were this person?

(a.)	pleased	d.	insulted	g.	embarrassed
b.	let down	(e.)	good	h.	surprised
c.	tolerated	(f.)	relieved	i.	angry

4. Drug Addict: "I guess when I was a teenager I felt so down all the time and speed made me feel better. I still like it, but I feel like the speed is in control, not me. I'm always hyper."

How would I feel if I were this person?

a.	uneasy	d.	good	(g.)	helpless
b.	excited	(e.)	scared	h.	potent
c.	confused	f.	turned on	(i.)	lost

5. Patient: "I got back the lab tests today—it's not cancer! I feel like life is beginning all over again! Fantastic!"

How would I feel if I were this person?

(a.)	relieved	d.	topsy-turvy	g.	free
b.	disappointed	(e.)	thrilled	h.	depressed
(c.)	alive	f.	foggy	i.	initiated

Introduction

This exercise is designed to help you generate a large number of feeling words. It can be used as a "think step" when you are stuck for a word to use when responding to a person.

Instructions

Take each of the stimulus words given and complete the sentence with another feeling word. Now, use the new word as your next stimulus and repeat the process.

Example

When I feel angry, I feel <u>furious</u>.

When I feel <u>furious</u>, I feel <u>burned</u>.

When I feel <u>burned</u>, I feel <u>cheated</u>.

When I feel <u>cheated</u>, I feel <u>hurt</u>.

When I feel <u>hurt,</u> I feel <u>sad</u>.

Exercise

1. What I feel excited, I feel ___*happy*___.

When I feel ___*happy*___, I feel ___*good*___.

When I feel ___*good*___, I feel ___*confident*___.

When I feel ___*confident*___, I feel ___*peaceful*___.

When I feel ___*peaceful*___, I feel ___*calm*___.

2. When I feel helpless, I feel _____ lost _____.

When I feel _____ lost _____, I feel _____ confused _____.

When I feel _____ confused _____, I feel _____ miserable _____.

When I feel _____ miserable _____, I feel _____ down _____.

When I feel _____ down _____, I feel _____ depressed _____.

3. When I feel afraid, I feel _____ scared _____.

When I feel _____ scared _____, I feel _____ vulnerable _____.

When I feel _____ vulnerable _____, I feel _____ insecure _____.

When I feel _____ insecure _____, I feel _____ anxious _____.

When I feel _____ anxious _____, I feel _____ powerless _____.

4. When I feel mixed up, I feel _____ confused _____.

When I feel _____ confused _____, I feel _____ insecure _____.

When I feel _____ insecure _____, I feel _____ insignificant _____.

When I feel _____ insignificant _____, I feel _____ worthless _____.

When I feel _____ worthless _____, I feel _____ hurt _____.

EXERCISE 27: ORGANIZING YOUR FEELING WORD VOCABULARY

Introduction

A feeling word chart will help you find feeling words as you complete this book and as you practice responding.

Instructions

Record the new feeling words you generated in Exercise 26 on the next page or on page 115 of *The Art of Helping*. Add any more new feeling words that you can think of.

FEELING WORD VOCABULARY LIST*

Levels of Intensity	Happy	Sad	Angry	Scared	Confused	Strong	Weak
High	Excited Elated Overjoyed *Ecstatic*	Hopeless Depressed Devastated *miserable* *hurt*	Furious Seething Enraged	Fearful Afraid Threatened	Bewildered Trapped Troubled *anxious* *torn*	Potent Super Powerful	Overwhelmed Impotent Vulnerable *powerless* *insignificant* *worthless*
Medium	Cheerful Up Good	Upset Distressed Sorry	Agitated Frustrated Irritated	Edgy Insecure Uneasy	Disorganized Mixed-Up Awkward *baffled*	Energetic Confident Capable	Incapable Helpless Insecure
Low	Glad Content Satisfied	Down Low Bad	Uptight Dismayed Annoyed	Timid Unsure Nervous	Bothered Uncomfortable Undecided *worried* *uncertain* *unsure*	Sure Secure Solid	Shaky Unsure Bored

*Since the intensity of any feeling word depends upon the person with whom it is used, you will need to visualize the typical helpee you work with to categorize these words by intensity level. (An Expanded Feeling Word List is found in Appendix A of *The Art of Helping* text.)

EXERCISE 28: PRACTICING FEELING RESPONSES

Introduction

The next exercise will help you learn to select an appropriate feeling word and use that word in a response to feeling.

Instructions

Imagine that you are listening to each of the people listed below. Try to respond interchangeably to the feelings expressed by each. Use your feeling word chart to find several words that fit the person.

Remember, the empathy question is, "How would I feel if I were *this person*?" not, "How would *I* feel in that situation?"

Example

Alcoholic: "Things are all straightened out with my daughter now. I explained to her about my drinking problem and why I have to go to those long meetings. It's still hard for her 'cause she's so young, but she understands a little better what Mommy needs to do to get well."

1. You feel <u>relieved</u>.

2. You feel <u>hopeful</u>.

Exercise

1. Student: "Here I am...again. It's mid-semester, and I'm way behind in all my work, just barely passing a couple of courses. It's like I can't think ahead—one of the guys will come in and want to party and I say sure, then the next day I realize I didn't finish a paper or something. I do the same thing every semester. What's wrong with me—can't I learn from my past?"

a. You feel _confused_

b. You feel _worried_

2. **Ex-wife:** "My ex-husband is driving me crazy. We got a divorce six years ago and now suddenly he wants to fight me for custody of the kids. I know he doesn't have a case, but he's hassling me just to get me mad."

   a. You feel _furious_

   b. You feel _irritated_

3. **Boyfriend:** "My girlfriend and I really get along pretty well, y'know. But lately, I just can't seem to...well, y'know..perform...in the bedroom. And she thinks it's her fault and I think it's my fault and we both end up getting really mad."

   a. You feel _frustrated_

   b. You feel _incapable_

4. **Adult Male:** "I'm just a three-quarters man. I've had so damn many opportunities in my life and I've thrown them all away."

   a. You feel _regretful_

   b. You feel _resentful_

5. **Young Woman:** "I'm really excited about this new job. I'm starting out at the bottom and the work is pretty dull right now but there's so much to learn! The potential for advancement is really good."

   a. You feel _hopeful_

   b. You feel _overjoyed_

Introduction

This exercise provides more practice in responding to feelings.

Instructions

Write your best feeling response to each of the statements below. Use the format, "You feel ," so that you have responses and not just a feeling word.

Example

Adolescent Girl: "My friends are really hassling me to do the same things they're doing. I don't want to smoke and drink—at least not yet—but I don't want to lose my friends either."

Response: You feel torn

Exercise

1. Young Adult: "I'm really confused. My friends tell me I'm very warm and outgoing and yet when I meet a new person I feel like I'm being really self-conscious and anxious."

   Response: _you feel mixed-up_

2. Father: "Do you know what it's like? Once I was on top of the world and then my daughter was killed...and I just fell apart. I keep saying— if only I hadn't let her take the car that night. It was raining, she was just a kid, just got her license. I should have driven her. I've got to live with this. And I can't."

   Response: _you feel devastated_

3. Business-woman: "The new job is really working out. I have responsibilities for supervision and for training. It's the right career track for me. Finally, I can invest myself—I'm doing something I feel good about."

Response: _you feel confident_

4. Welfare Client: "The hell with it! I've had it with you damn social workers and your do-good agencies."

Response: _you feel furious_

5. Nurse: "Mrs. Jones just kept crying and crying. It's so terrible when a child dies. No one knows what to do or say to comfort the parents. It's the really painful part of my work."

Response: _you feel powerless_

EXERCISE 30: PRACTICING RESPONDING TO TWO FEELINGS

Introduction

Sometimes the person will express two conflicting feelings. To respond effectively you must be able to identify how the combination of the two feelings makes the person feel.

Instructions

In the following responses, identify the two feelings present and then develop a response that accurately captures the whole feeling. To do this exercise successfully, ask yourself:

- *How do I feel when I feel _____ and _____?*

Now use this feeling word to formulate a response to the helpee:

- Response: *You feel _____.*

Example

Parent: "I don't want to fight with my kids all the time. I know I am responsible for giving them direction and helping them make wise decisions. But it is such a battle sometimes, I feel like giving up."

1. *How do I feel when I feel <u>responsible</u> and <u>fed up</u>?*

2. Response: You feel <u>discouraged</u>.

Exercise

1. Veteran: "This position would offer me more money plus good benefits and a 30% of profits bonus. I think I should take it. But it doesn't really fit into my career plans and I'm not that interested in selling tires. Like you said, though, right now I need something to get me back on my feet, and the job is good for that."

 a. *How do I feel when I feel _____ and _____?*

 b. Response: You feel _____.

68

2. Wife: "How could he treat me that way! I've been good to him—generous, respectful. I've really been the perfect person. And now he tells me we're through. Walking out! It's not right! How dare he leave me alone after so many years?"

a.   *How do I feel when I feel* _____ *and* _____?

b.   Response: You feel _____.

3. Supervisor: "The guy was a real loser. I mean, give some people responsibility and they just blow it. This guy just couldn't handle being account-able. I promoted him and what does he do? Quits one month later And now the boss is down on my neck because I'm the one who promoted him. My boss says I showed bad business judgment."

a.   *How do I feel when I feel* _____ *and* _____?

b.   Response: You feel _____.

4. Professor: "It's difficult to tell whether to believe her or not. My gut impulse is that she's lying. She did cheat—the answers just don't reflect her, the way she presents herself. I didn't actually see anything. I'm suspicious but I don't have any concrete evidence."

a.   *How do I feel when I feel* _____ *and* _____?

b.   Response: You feel _____.

5. Husband: "If she doesn't like it—she will just have to live with it. I'm through changing who I am. Trying to match some picture in her head of 'Macho Man.' She may not want me then. But that's a risk I've got to take. I've got to find out or it'll destroy me. Don't you think I'm right? Isn't it time to find out if she has room for me? If she doesn't... maybe...but maybe she does."

a.   *How do I feel when I feel* _____ *and* _____?

b.   Response: You feel _____.

RESPONDING TO MEANING

OVERVIEW

A response to meaning communicates an understanding of the full experience of the helpee: an understanding of both the feeling and the reason for it.

Example

Dorm Resident: "I just don't understand it. I walked into my room this afternoon and my roommate totally ignored me! I asked her what was wrong, she looked at me and said, 'You should know," then left. I felt about an inch tall. And no one else will tell me anything either. What am I supposed to do if no one will let me in on it?"

Response: "You feel bewildered because no one's giving you any clues as to why your roommate is so upset."

This response combines the two responses you have already practiced, responding to content and to feeling. Review *The Art of Helping*, pages 117–123 for an explanation of this skill.

EXERCISE 31: DISCRIMINATING INTERCHANGEABLE RESPONSES

Introduction

If you have the ability to recognize good and bad responses, you will be able to give yourself feedback on your own future responses and improve your responding skills.

Instructions

Select the response(s) that are interchangeable for each statement. When a response is *not* interchangeable, identify the errors in the response.

Remember, some typical errors are:

- Content *too long* (keep responses brief)
- Content *parroted* (paraphrase your responses)
- Content too *vague* (be specific)
- Feeling *category* inaccurate

- Feeling *intensity* inaccurate
- Feeling word *inappropriate* for the person being responded to
- Feeling *experience* is described ("feel that", "feel like") no feeling *word* is included
- Content *not interchangeable* (adds or subtracts content, judgmental)

Example

Job Hunter: "Most employees want managers to be tough. You're supposed to jump on people all the time. I'm just not that way."

a. You feel <u>frustrated</u> because <u>employers look for a quality in their managers that you don't have</u>.

Error(s):   <u>None, interchangeable</u>   .

b. You feel <u>good</u> because <u>you are different.</u>

Error(s):   <u>Wrong category feeling, content too vague</u>   .

c. You feel <u>scared</u> because <u>no one will hire you as a manager</u>.

Error(s):   <u>Wrong intensity feeling; not interchangeable—adds content</u>   .

d. You feel <u>like you're being blocked</u> because <u>employers ask for managers to be tougher than you are.</u>

Error(s):   <u>No feeling word—experience only</u>   .

e. You feel <u>discouraged</u> because <u>the business world is such a dog-eat-dog place</u>.

Error(s):   <u>Content not interchangeable</u>   .

Exercise

1. Boss: "I'm fed up! No one around here takes me seriously. The next person who comes in late is fired and I mean it."

   a. You feel <u>appalled</u> because <u>people don't believe you'll act on what you threaten.</u>

      Error(s): _wrong category feeling, add content_.

   b. You feel <u>mad</u> because <u>employees are no good these days.</u>

      Error(s): _Not interchangeable, wrong feeling intensity_.

   c. You feel <u>irritated</u> because <u>people don't pay any attention to what you say.</u>

      Error(s): _None; interchangeable_.

   d. You feel <u>confused</u> because <u>the people here don't listen to you.</u>

      Error(s): _Wrong category feeling, adds content_.

   e. You feel <u>angry</u> because <u>of this.</u>

      Error(s): _Too vague (content)_.

2. Seamstress: "Hey, this is really excellent. The quality of this material is exactly what I've been looking for. Now, I can finish my suit."

   a. You feel <u>pleased</u> that <u>the material is good.</u>

      Error(s): _wrong feeling intensity, content to vague_.

   b. You feel that <u>the material is perfect for your suit.</u>

      Error(s): _No feeling word_.

   c. You feel <u>thrilled</u> because <u>the quality of the material is exactly what you've been looking for</u>. Now, you can finish your suit.

      Error(s): _Parrots back what was said. wrong feeling intensity_.

   d. You feel <u>hopeful</u> because <u>this material is of such high quality</u>. It's quite excellent material and because the material is so good, you can complete the suit you've been working on. You've been looking for material like this so it's really great to find it.

      Error(s): _wrong categoring feeling. Content too long Adds content_.

   e. You feel <u>happy</u> because <u>the material is excellent for completing your suit.</u>

      Error(s): _None, interchangeable_.

72

Introduction

This exercise gives you time to generate a quality response to meaning. Writing your responses will help you build experience for the future when you will need to respond verbally and "in-the-moment."

Instructions

Write your best responses to each of the statements below using the format:
"You feel _____ because _____."

Example

Woman: "I went to visit an older friend in the hospital yesterday. We had a really good visit. I hugged her when we said hello and she just started crying. I think she needed to do that. I guess my visit made a difference to her."

You feel <u>pleased</u> because <u>you were able to help a friend</u>.

Exercise

1. Dorm Resident: "My roommate is such a selfish person, I don't think he ever had to think of anyone else in his life—everything in *our* room is organized *his* way."

   <u>You feel annoyed because your friend is inconsiderate</u>

2. Friend: "She's going nuts, I think. Last night out of the blue she sent everyone home. I mean nothing happened, it was just suddenly she wanted to be alone."

   <u>you feel baffled because you do not understand what's going on with your friend</u>

3. Young Adult: "I have a really hard time determining my career values. I want a good living but it's gotta be something that makes me feel proud and makes me feel like I'm contributing something to other people. A job like teaching or social work is too much self-sacrifice for me, though."

you feel uncertain because you haven't figured out completely what you want to do for a career

4. Alcoholic: "I haven't held a job in more than one year. I'm a good employee, and do high quality work when I'm sober. But all these employers—it doesn't matter to them, the minute they find out I drink, even if never do on the job, they let me go."

you feel disappointed because your alcoholism has cost you several jobs.

5. Drug Abuser: "They keep telling you, 'No drugs,' but this damn place is like a prison. Using drugs is the only way to stand it."

you feel

6. Teenager: "I don't see what's so wrong with it. A little grass is like a drink and you see plenty of people drinking. The same old characters that tell me I'll 'fry my brains' are soaking their brains in alcohol."

7. Middle-aged Adult: "I'm just so down these days. I look back to when I was young—you know, high school, college. I seemed to be so hopeful. But now it just seems like years since I felt so good. And yet what's missing? I've got my family, a house, a good job, and some regular people in my life. What is it, what's missing?"

you feel confused because you do not understand why you are unhappy

8. Patient:

"I've been sitting here waiting for three hours now—these emergency rooms are impossible. No one talks to you or tells you what's going on. You just sit and wait."

you feel frustrated because you are being ignored

9. Factory Worker:

"I've been very happy working with this company. I've learned a great deal. I feel like I'm a real worker and I'd like to apply for a promotion now."

you feel confident because you feel you are capable and ready for a promotion

10. Client:

"Your advice was really bad. I went in and told my supervisor how I thought he could become more productive. You know what he said—I should stick to my own job and not get a swelled head."

you feel annoyed because my advice turned out to be rotten

EXERCISE 33: RESPONDING TO TWO THEMES

Introduction

Sometimes a person expresses two themes. A good helper can accurately combine them into one meaning response.

Instructions

Write your best response to each statement below. In Exercise 28 you practiced responding to feeling. Now, combine the two themes appropriately so that your response to meaning expresses one feeling and one content.

Example

Adult: "I've been really looking forward to meeting him. I've heard so much about him. He seems really nice, yet there's a feeling of 'watch out!' He could get nasty."

You feel <u>anxious</u> because <u>he gives you two messages—nice and nasty</u>.

Exercise

1. Adult: "Sometimes it's such a struggle. I work and work to get where I'm going and every step is hard. Yet, there can be weeks at a time when my life just flows—I get the Midas touch."

You feel _____ because _____

_____

2. Wife: "My husband can be so mature and responsible. He can attend to details and impress me. I get really made when he behaves like a child, it's so out of the blue."

You feel _____ because _____

_____

3. Teacher: "This child is a mystery to me. No matter what I do the child is always calm and courteous. What a treat! And impressive. I get suspicious of it though—what child can be so perfect? And then I think, 'No, it's my teacher's mind.' We get so used to the bad ones we think they're all that way."

You feel _____ because _____

_____

4. Doctor: "The signs of illness are really unclear. The patient's breathing and eyes are good, no fever, nothing. Yet, he seems to have a long-term cough."

You feel _____ because _____

_____

5. Husband: "I'd like to be there if she needs me. But this is the fourth operation this summer and every time I come with her, I miss work—and pay. I know that we need the money to afford this medical care, but I don't want her to be alone."

You feel _____ because _____

_____

EXERCISE 34: RESPONDING TO YOURSELF

Introduction

Up to this point you have been practicing with a variety of helpees—but no live ones. To help you make the transition from these written helpees to a live person, the following exercise will give you a chance to help yourself.

Responding to yourself will give you an opportunity to begin working with a live helpee whom you know very well. Familiarity makes responding easier. You will also get an idea of what it is like to be a helpee.

Instructions

Fill in the information requested.

Exercise

1a. Write a brief paragraph describing some current experience in your life as a learner.

Recently, I have been unmotivated to go to school. I know it is important for me to go but lately I cannot convince myself. I'm afraid that if I continue like this, my grades will all go down and I'll fall apart

1b. Respond to how you feel and why.

I feel _____incapable_____ because _____I cannot get myself motivated._____

78

2a. Write a brief paragraph describing something you are pleased with in your home life.

> I always look forward to the comfort of my room. There I feel at peace with myself. At home, on my bed, I feel safe and secure and I never have to worry about anything other than myself.

2b. Respond to how you feel and why.

I feel _____secure_____ because _____I have a place where I always belong_____

3a. Write a brief paragraph describing something you would like to change in your work setting.

> Work hasn't been great lately. I keep getting passed on from one room to the next. They never ask my opinion about any decisions, we have to make. They decide everything and order me around like I'm some sort of a puppet. They really need to be more considerate about their employees

3b. Respond to how you feel and why.

I feel _____fed up_____ because _____the place where I work is inconsiderate of its employees_____

EXERCISE 35: VIDEO EXERCISE—RESPONDING SKILLS

Introduction

This exercise will give you an opportunity to identify interchangeable responses to meaning. You will also get a chance to write your own interchangeable responses.

Instructions

Read the following exercise then view the videotape *"Responding Skills."* You will need to attend, observe and listen closely. The two graduate students present their problems to Dr. Carkhuff and he responds to them. Identify at least two interchangeable responses that Dr. Carkhuff makes and paraphrase what he says in the space provided.

1. _____

   _____

2. _____

   _____

3. Now write your own interchangeable response to Lin.

   You feel _____ because _____

   _____

4. Formulate an interchangeable response to Don.

   You feel _____ because _____

   _____

4. PERSONALIZING—FACILITATING HELPEE UNDERSTANDING

OVERVIEW

You have learned to attend to another person's experience by attending physically, observing, and listening. You have also learned to respond accurately and interchangeably to the feeling and content that the person expressed. Now you will learn to *personalize* the person's experience. Personalizing helps a person to gain control of a situation so that he or she can act on the experience.*

Personalizing involves building an interchangeable base, personalizing the meaning, personalizing the problem, personalizing the goal, and personalizing changing feelings so the person can identify where he or she is in relation to where he or she wants to be. An example of the personalizing process is given below. The exercises following it will take you through each step of personalizing.

Before you do any of these exercises, read Chapter 6 of *The Art of Helping* (pages 131–179) to learn about personalizing.

Example

The following dialogue illustrates the steps of personalizing.

Building an Interchangeable Base

Patient:	"No one's told me a thing. I feel like I'm just a disease lying here! No person—at least, no one treats me like they see me!"
Response:	You feel annoyed because the people here ignore you.
Patient:	"Ignore me? They avoid me! I'm not even aware of what's wrong with me. If I paid attention to the way they treat me, I'd think I had leprosy."
Response:	You feel angry because they act like it'll harm them to approach you.
Patient:	"It wouldn't take much. A little decency. I don't want them to betray information...I just want to be seen...and spoken to."
Response:	You feel lonely because no one talks to you.

*For additional information about personalizing problems and goals, see Carkhuff, R.R. *Human Possibilities— Human Capital in the 21st Century*. Amherst, MA: HRD Press, 2000.

Patient:	"I've been here two weeks now and it's like living in prison—cold and sterile, being all alone with no control."
Response:	You feel anxious because the staff is in charge—totally.
Patient:	"If I just knew what was wrong. They clam up when they're around me and it's scaring me. What does it mean?"
Response:	You feel frightened because they seem to be hiding something bad from you.
Patient:	"I had this real bad pain in my head and then seemed to black out. So my family brought me in. We were scared...a brain tumor. The doctor says 'no'...but what?"
Response:	You feel lost because there has not been a clear diagnosis.

Personalizing Meaning

Patient:	"I try to ask but I get so...(pause) maybe I'm happier not knowing. But I wish I knew—it's my body, maybe my life."
Response:	You feel scared because you're left not knowing what's going on.
Patient:	"And I don't know why I don't just ask the doctor outright. I'm stuck. I don't think that I can overcome this fear. What if I can't handle the bad news?"
Response:	You feel afraid because you believe that you might "fall apart" emotionally if the doctor's news is real bad.

Personalized Problem

Patient:	"Yeah, I'm terrified...and my terror keeps me ignorant! I'm feeling like I'm just lying here waiting for the boom to strike."
Response:	You feel vulnerable because you can't act unless you know what's wrong, and, right now, you can't get the information from your doctor that you need.

Personalized Feeling

Patient:	"I can't act, I can't even get up the nerve to ask the doc to tell me the truth."
Response:	You feel frustrated with yourself because you can't ask the doctor what's wrong.

Personalized Goal

Patient: "And it's making me sicker. I'm scared...(pause) but I've got to find out."

Response: You feel desperate because you can't help yourself without the information and you know that you need to ask the doctor what's wrong with you.

Personalized Feeling

Patient: "Yea, I do...I have to. I need to prepare myself for what he might say.... Even if it's bad news I'll get some relief just knowing."

Response: You feel anxious to find out because you're knowing may lead to some sense of relief from the terror of the unknown.

EXERCISE 36: EXPLORING PERSONALIZING SKILLS

Introduction

This exercise will help you to understand the importance of personalizing skills for effective helping.

Instructions

Think back to the last time that someone gave you some information that helped you to understand what you needed to do to solve a problem. Then, answer the following questions and fill in any information.

Exercises

1. What was it about the person or your relationship to him or her that made you accept and use the information that he or she gave you?

_____

_____

_____

_____

_____

_____

_____

_____

_____

2. Did the person help you to identify your role in the situation?

    ☐   Yes   ☐   No

3. Did the person help you to see what you were doing that made the problem worse?

    ☐   Yes   ☐   No

4. Did you have a goal after talking to this person?

    ☐   Yes   ☐   No

5. Why are these things helpful?

   a. Showing you that your point of view was understood

   _____

   _____

   _____

   _____

   b. Helping you to identify your role in the situation

   _____

   _____

   _____

   _____

   c. Helping you to identify what you were doing that made the problem worse

   _____

   _____

   _____

   _____

   d. Helping you to develop a goal

   _____

   _____

   _____

   _____

EXERCISE 37: BUILDING AN INTERCHANGEABLE BASE

Introduction

If you are going to employ personalizing skills effectively, you must first be able to facilitate the helpee to sustain his or her exploration. This means that you must be able to make multiple interchangeable responses to the helpee to build an interchangeable base of empathic responsiveness.

Instructions

Below is a series of exploratory comments made by two different people. After each statement, write an interchangeable response to meaning (feeling and content).

Example

Refer to the examples in Exercise 32 for samples of interchangeable responses.

Exercise

1. **Student**

    a. "That damn teacher! She doesn't even look at my work. Her comments are so ridiculous. And she's picky about such little things, misspelled words and poor handwriting. Those have nothing to do with what I know about a subject."

    _____

    _____

    _____

    b. "Like this paper I just got back—no grade! She wants me to correct it before she grades the content. Imagine! So what if I can't spell!"

    _____

    _____

    _____

    c. "I haven't got time to go back and rewrite papers or type them. She said something in class about a standard of excellence and attention to detail being part of that. I always thought my standard was good enough—I get by, don't I?"

    _____

    _____

    _____

d. "And getting the broad perspective is more important than detail. Detail stuff is just nit-picking. My work is good enough for everyone else—I get my C's."

_____

_____

_____

e. "Who does she think I am? I'm just an average person. I probably could do better, but is it worth it? I'm pretty happy now, except for people like her pushing me."

_____

_____

_____

f. "All my life people have been on my back. Oh, not everybody, but my dad was that way and a lot of bosses I've had. People like her think that just because their label puts them in charge everyone had better dance to their tune. I won't!"

_____

_____

_____

2. **Wife**

a. "I don't know what's wrong between my husband and me. When we got married we were so close and now there's a void between us. We just don't communicate."

_____

_____

_____

b. "We used to tell each other everything. It's not that we're hiding any-thing from each other—I'm not and I'm sure he isn't, but I don't know what he's doing, what he's thinking."

_____

_____

_____

c. "It feels almost like we're living in separate worlds. We just kind of touch each other in passing. I'm busy, he's busy...y'know, we used to put each other first but now everything else seems to get put ahead of 'us'."

_____

_____

_____

d. "We didn't mean to let things get like this. He doesn't say anything but I know he's as worried about this gap as I am. Thinking about it, he probably doesn't have any more idea of where I am now than I have of where he is."

_____

_____

_____

e. "Things just slipped away without either of us noticing. Time kind of got out of control—all these things that take you away from what really matters."

_____

_____

_____

f. "It's funny how little time we give to what matters most. I wonder if we could get it back, be close again?"

_____

_____

_____

EXERCISE 38: RESPONDING TO THE COMMON THEME

Introduction

Over a period of time, you may find that a helpee is expressing a common theme. You may recognize a theme by its recurrence. It is important that we show our understanding to the helpee by responding to the theme expressed. This means communicating a response that summarizes both the helpee's feeling (from the helpee's multiple expressions of feeling) and the reason for this feeling (from the helpee's multiple expressions of content).

You may want to read page 140 of *The Art of Helping* before completing this exercise.

Instructions

For each of the following helpee statements, write a response that is interchangeable to the theme expressed by the helpee.

Example

Adolescent (11 years old):	"Well, here I am in this new house. But Jimmy, my best friend, is not around. All my other friends are gone, too. And, I can't go down by the river anymore, either."
Response to Theme:	"You feel sad because a lot of important people and places have been left behind."

Exercise

1. Teenager: "I can't wait to get a car of my own so I can go where I want and when I want. I need more spending money, too. It would be good if I had a part-time job. (Pause) And I want to move my bedroom to the loft over the garage. I don't know if my parents are ready for any of this, but I'm sure ready."

Response to Theme: _____

_____

_____

2. Young Adult: "Art, I love art. I've been talking about taking a night class at the Community College but.... And, I owe a lot of people letters. It seems that I just don't get around to writing them. (pause) And someday I'm going to go rafting down the Colorado River. That will be a great trip."

Response to Theme: _____

_____

_____

3. Adult: "Oh, yes, I've had a garden for many years. It's good to get dirt under your fingers and to fill up your senses with the smell of the earth. (With eyes opened wide and smiling) And whenever possible, we go to the woodlands and take a walk along the streams and up the mountains. We've done this many times."

Response to Theme: _____

_____

_____

4. Young Adult: "And who is looking out for me? Not my parents. Not my supposed friends. Nobody at work. Who?"

Response to Theme: _____

_____

_____

5. Child
(8 years old):   "About two or three times a year we go up to visit my cousins, Amy, Andrew and Michael. We have a lot of fun at their house. Uncle Paul and Auntie Joanne take us on boat rides and we go swimming in a lake and everything."

Response to Theme: _____

_____

_____

PERSONALIZING MEANING

OVERVIEW

When helpees talk about how other people and outside events impact their lives, they are *externalizing* about their experiences. When helpees talk about themselves, about what they are doing or not doing, about why they are feeling and acting the way they are, they are *internalizing* or personalizing their experiences.

All personalizing is about internalizing. When helpers formulate and communicate any personalized response, the helpers are adding information so the helpees can better understand their experiences and their roles in their experiences.

When helpers formulate and communicate responses that personalize meaning for the helpees, the helper responses add to the helpees' understanding of why their experiences are important. Personalized meaning responses may be formulated and communicated to add to the helpees' understanding of the implications or consequences of their roles in their experiences. Personalized meaning responses may also be formulated and communicated to add to the helpees' understanding of their assumptions or beliefs about their situations.

To check your understanding of personalizing meaning, review *The Art of Helping*, pages 146–150.

Example

Adult:

"I've got some terrific ideas for starting a new business. But, my bankers won't give me a loan to get started. They don't value ideas. They only value things, like real estate and cash. They don't understand me."

Interchangeable Response to Meaning:

"You feel upset because your bank is being so narrow-minded."

NOTE: The focus of this interchangeable response to meaning (feeling and content) is external. Someone other than the helpee is seen as the reason for the feeling—"my bank won't give me a loan."

Personalized Meaning Response:

> "You feel angry because you spend so much time looking for a loan when you could be doing other important things."

> **NOTE:** The focus of this personalized response to meaning is internal. It also goes beyond what the helper has said. It explores the implications or consequences of the helpee's behavior for the helpee.

Personalized Meaning Response:

> "You feel confident because you believe that you will find a way to obtain the necessary financing."

> **NOTE:** The focus of this personalized response to meaning is also internal. It also goes beyond what the helper has said. It explores one of the helpee's assumptions or beliefs about his or her behavior.

EXERCISE 39: DISCRIMINATING PERSONALIZED MEANING

Introduction

In this exercise you will practice discriminating interchangeable responses from personalized meaning responses.

Instructions

Identify which of the responses are interchangeable responses (IR) to the helpee's expression and which responses personalize the meaning (PM). Remember that an interchangeable responses (IR) to meaning expresses how something or someone else is causing the helpee to feel the way he or she feels (externalizing). A personalized meaning (PM) response expresses the helpee's role in his or her experience (internalizing). Write *IR* for interchangeable response or *PM* for personalized meaning in the blank preceding each response.

Review page 136 in *The Art of Helping* before completing this exercise.

Example

Father: "I've been sitting here waiting for three hours now—these emergency rooms are impossible. No one talks to you or tells you what's going on. You just sit and wait."

___IR___ a. You feel frustrated because no one pays any attention to you.

___IR___ b. You feel anxious because they've kept you waiting for three hours without saying why.

___PM___ c. You feel scared because you have no control of the situation.

Exercise

1. Working Student: "I'm so tired, I don't know what to do. I try to keep up with everything: work, home, classes. But each day seems so long. By noon, I'm already too tired to cope."

_____ a. You feel discouraged because you've lost your edge.

_____ b. You feel tired because there's so much to do.

_____ c. You feel tired because you lack the energy to do it all.

2. Employee: "Damn! I blew it again. I just don't seem to be able to think before I open my big mouth. This job was going so smoothly before I got mad and told off my supervisor."

_____ a. You feel angry because you keep repeating your mistakes.

_____ b. You feel upset because this situation is happening again.

_____ c. You feel down because you really thought you were going to make it on this job.

3. Special Ed Teacher: "The teacher's aide I got this year is a real winner. She acts like she's 14—and that's being kind. I don't know how I'm gonna make it through the year with her."

_____ a. You feel annoyed because she's as bad as one of the kids.

_____ b. You feel angry because you're going to have to cope with an added problem.

_____ c. You feel frustrated because she isn't mature enough to cope with the class.

4. Welfare Recipient: "I'm just a three-quarters man. I've had so damn many opportunities in my life and I've thrown them all away."

_____ a. You feel down because you've lost every opportunity.

_____ b. You feel depressed because opportunities never work out for you.

_____ c. You feel sad because you never made anything of yourself.

EXERCISE 40: PRACTICING PERSONALIZED
MEANING RESPONSES

Introduction

This exercise will help you learn to make your own personalized meaning responses after you have made an interchangeable response to meaning.

Instructions

For each of the following helpee statements, write two responses. First write an interchangeable response to meaning. Second, write a personalized response to meaning that *adds* to the helpee's understanding. Remember, a good response is brief and specific.

Example

1. Roommate: "I don't know what he expects, but I know what I want. I want things my way for once. I'm tired of always having to make room for everyone else but never having anyone leave room for who I am."

a. Response to meaning: You feel <u>angry</u>
because <u>he doesn't acknowledge your needs</u>.

b. Response to personalized meaning: You feel <u>determined</u>
because you <u>plan to assert your own needs</u>.

Exercise

1. College Student: "What I do is good enough. I'm happy with my life, except for people pushing me to do better. Why? All my life people have been on my back. Oh, not everybody, but my dad was that way, and a lot of bosses I've had. They think their label allows them to make everyone dance to their tune. And I won't!"

   a. Response to meaning: You feel _____

       because _____ .

   b. Response to personalized meaning:

       You feel _____

       because you _____

       _____ .

2. Husband: "Things just slipped away without either of us noticing. Time kind of got out of control—all those little things that take you away from what really matters. Funny how little time we give to what matters most. I wonder if we could get it back, be close again?"

   a. Response to meaning: You feel _____

       because _____ .

   b. Response to personalized meaning:

       You feel _____

       because you _____

       _____ .

3. Teenager: "I know I could solve my problems; they aren't that heavy, just annoying. I'm not real thrilled with being back in school, but I want to do well. Yet I party almost every night, drink too much, can't get up for classes, get more behind, then feel bad about it, so what do I do? I go out drinking again."

   a.   Response to meaning: You feel _____

       because _____.

   b.   Response to personalized meaning:

       You feel _____

       because you _____

       _____.

4. Probationer: "Why am I here? This wasn't *my* idea, I'm not 'sick' or anything. The court says 'you go see a counselor and we'll suspend your sentence.' So here I am, but there's nothing you can do for me if nothing's wrong. None of the others did anything...why should this be different?"

   a.   Response to meaning: You feel _____

       because _____.

   b.   Response to personalized meaning:

       You feel _____

       because you _____

       _____.

PERSONALIZING PROBLEMS

OVERVIEW

Personalizing the problem requires identifying what the person *cannot do* that is contributing to the problem.*

Example

Sister: "They talk about her like she isn't there. It really bothers me when I don't interfere—I'm older, I could protect her. I want to do it right though, and I never know what to say, how to handle it!"

Personalized Problem:

You feel badly because <u>you cannot</u> handle the people who attack her.

Review pages 151–161 in *The Art of Helping* before doing the following exercises.

EXERCISE 41: DISCRIMINATING PERSONALIZED PROBLEM RESPONSES

Introduction

In this exercise you will practice discriminating personalized problem (PP) response from personalized meaning (PM) responses and interchangeable responses to meaning (IR).

Instructions

Read the statements and responses below and identify the responses as:

__IR__   Interchangeable response to meaning: "You feel _____

because _____."

__PM__   Personalized meaning: "You feel _____

because you _____."

__PP__   Personalized problem: "You feel _____

because you cannot _____."

*For additional information about personalizing problems and goals, see Carkhuff, R.R. *Human Possibilities—Human Capital in the 21st Century*. Amherst, MA: HRD Press, 2000.

Example

Middle-Aged Husband:		"I know I've got to handle this myself. It really gets me down, watching my wife go back to drinking. But I can't join her. I've got to be strong enough to say no. It's my only chance—and if I can beat it, maybe I can help her."

__IR__   a. You feel saddened because your wife is destroying herself.

__PM__   b. You feel alone because you're the only one you can count on.

__PP__   c. You feel inadequate because you cannot help your wife before you help yourself.

Exercise

1. Young Adult: "I guess when I was a teenager I felt so down all the time and the speed made me feel better. But now, the speed is running me; I'm out of control and yet I keep on taking it."

_____   a. You feel scared because you cannot break your speed habit.

_____   b. You feel uneasy because the speed is in control.

_____   c. You feel helpless because you've given up control of your life.

2. Lower Management Employee: "They really use me in that store. I do everything and I just don't think anybody notices. Oh, maybe they do...but I don't really fit in...that's what it is. They'll never promote me. I'm too unique. I have to speak up when things seem wrong to me."

_____   a. You feel irritated because they don't appreciate your value to them.

_____   b. You feel discouraged because you don't fit what they're looking for.

_____   c. You feel frustrated because you cannot get promoted when you voice your own opinion the way you do.

3. 21-Year-Old: "My boyfriend wants me to live with him. He keeps mentioning it and I keep saying no. I'm not really sure why not...and so I can't make it clear to him. He gets hurt... disappointed. I don't want that to happen, but I know I'm not ready to live with him."

_____ a. You feel conflicted because you aren't sure of your reasons for saying no.

_____ b. You feel bad because he gets disappointed by your refusal.

_____ c. You feel distressed because you can't explain—or fully understand yourself—where you're at.

4. 30-Year-Old Husband: "I don't really know what I want to do with my marriage. I want to be fair to my wife but I don't know if I love her or not. It's really strange. I'm half married, half single."

_____ a. You feel depressed because you can't decide whether to make a commitment to your marriage or get out.

_____ b. You feel bothered because your marriage is so unsettled.

_____ c. You feel tormented because you are cheating your wife, your marriage—and yourself—by your indecision.

EXERCISE 42: PRACTICING PERSONALIZING PROBLEMS

Introduction

Now you are ready to formulate personalized problem responses of your own.

Instructions

Write three responses to each helpee excerpt: (1) write an interchangeable response to meaning, (2) write a response to the personalized meaning, and (3) write a response to the personalized problem.

Example

Young Man: "This diet doesn't work either. I've been trying to lose weight for, well, it seems like forever. I get fired up every time I start a new diet but I never stick it out. Even if I lose some weight I can't keep it off."

1. Interchangeable—You feel <u>discouraged</u> because <u>the diet</u> <u>doesn't work</u>

2. Personalized meaning—You feel <u>frustrated</u> because you <u>don't stick</u> <u>with your diets</u>

3. Personalized problem—You feel <u>disappointed</u> because you <u>cannot</u> <u>commit yourself to losing weight permanently</u>

Exercise

1. Wife: "I'm hurt. I gave 25 years to my marriage with him and now it's over. I feel cheated. I'm an old woman now. I thought my life would be all settled at this point. I never expected to be starting over. It hurts so much...I don't know if I can even do it."

   a. Interchangeable—You feel _____ because _____

   _____

   b. Personalized meaning—You feel _____ because you

   _____

   c. Personalized problem—You feel _____ because you cannot

   _____

2. Lower-Income Man: "I've tried calling and calling...at least 10 doctors. None of them will give me an appointment. First they ask if I have Blue Cross/Blue Shield—I don't—and then they give me an appointment in a month and a half. I've got to see someone; the doctors at the clinic couldn't tell me anything and no one will give me an appointment."

a. Interchangeable—You feel _____ because _____

_____

b. Personalized meaning—You feel _____ because you

_____

c. Personalized problem—You feel _____ because you cannot

_____

3. Mental Patient: "This staff here...they don't like me. I want to go home. But they tell me I'm crazy. I have to stay until they say I'm okay and I miss my home."

a. Interchangeable—You feel _____ because _____

_____

b. Personalized meaning—You feel _____ because you

_____

c. Personalized problem—You feel _____ because you cannot

_____

4. Parent: "My son is at it again. He's thirty-two years old and has a family of his own but he can't stop drinking booze. His wife tossed him out and he's been staying with us. But we're not young anymore. He's been drinking around here, too. He denies it but we know it's true. What can we do?"

a. Interchangeable—You feel _____ because _____

_____

b. Personalized meaning—You feel _____ because you

_____

c. Personalized problem—You feel _____ because you cannot

_____

PERSONALIZING GOALS

OVERVIEW

Personalizing the goal is the step that establishes where the helpee wants to be in relation to where he or she is. Before completing the next three exercises, review *The Art of Helping*, pages 156–161.

EXERCISE 43: DISCRIMINATING PERSONALIZED GOAL BEHAVIOR

Introduction

This exercise will help you learn to identify whether or not the goal is consistent with and appropriate for the problem. Goal behavior is defined as the *flip-side* of the problem behavior.

Instructions

Read the helpee excerpt then read each of the helper responses. Each helper response is an attempt to personalize a goal for the helpee. As you will see, the first half of the response is a description of the helpee's problem. The second half of the response is a description of the helpee's goal. Effective personalized goals flow directly from the personalized problem. They are the *flip-side* of the problem. In other words, the second half of the response is the *flip-side* of the first half of the response. Ineffective personalized goals do not flow directly from the personalized problem. Instead, they introduce new behaviors. To complete the exercise, label each response according to how the goal was developed: *flip-side* (directly related to the description of the problem) or new behavior (not directly related to the description of the problem).

Example

High School Athlete: "You never give me a chance. You always pick someone else. I don't count with you."

You feel discouraged because you can't find a way to be a part of the group and you want to belong.

| ✓ | Flip-side | | | New Behavior |

You feel discouraged because you can't find a way to be a part of the group and you need to open up more.

| | Flip-side | | ✓ | New Behavior |

103

Exercise

1. High School   "I try so hard to keep up in class. I do all the homework
   Math Student: and everything. But the stuff is boring, and way above
       my head."

   a. You feel worried because you can't do the work and you want to be able
   to make the Dean's list.

   ☐   Flip-side   ☐   New Behavior

   b. You feel helpless because you can't handle the material and you want
   very much to be able to deal with it.

   ☐   Flip-side   ☐   New Behavior

   c. You feel upset because you can't learn this subject and you really want
   an easier course.

   ☐   Flip-side   ☐   New Behavior

2. Worker: "I don't know if I want this new job. The money's better,
       but I'd have to deal with a whole different group of people
       who may not give me the support that I have here."

   a. You feel vulnerable because you don't have the responses to deal with
   the new people and you want to learn them.

   ☐   Flip-side   ☐   New Behavior

   b. You feel unsure because you can't decide about the new job and you
   want to make a decision you'll feel good about.

   ☐   Flip-side   ☐   New Behavior

   c. You feel lost because you can't deal with new people effectively and you
   want the new job to go well.

   ☐   Flip-side   ☐   New Behavior

3. Employee: "I'm so angry. First they tell me one thing, then they change the rules. I just don't seem to be able to say 'enough is enough.'"

a. You feel disappointed because you can't end the game-playing and you want to be a winner for a change.

☐ Flip-side   ☐ New Behavior

b. You feel disgusted with yourself because you can't take a firm stand and you want to be able to.

☐ Flip-side   ☐ New Behavior

c. You feel disgusted because you can't stand up for your rights and you want to take one of those assertiveness courses.

☐ Flip-side   ☐ New Behavior

4. Young Husband: "My wife is always nagging. Nothing I do is right anymore. It's *bitch* if I come home late and *bitch* if I come home early, and forbid the thought that I should mention her shortcomings!"

a. You feel sad because you don't know how to break out of the destructive pattern you're in and you want to break the cycle.

☐ Flip-side   ☐ New Behavior

b. You feel helpless because you can't get your wife to understand you and you want to be able to do what you want.

☐ Flip-side   ☐ New Behavior

c. You feel trapped because you can't communicate with your wife anymore and you really want to be able to talk with each other again.

☐ Flip-side   ☐ New Behavior

EXERCISE 44: DISCRIMINATING PERSONALIZED GOALS

Introduction

In the following exercise you will practice discriminating interchangeable responses (IR) to meaning, personalized meaning (PM) responses, personalized problem (PP) responses, and personalized goal (PG) responses.

Instructions

After the following excerpts you will find five responses. Read each response and identify what type of response it is. Label all five responses. Each responses will be one of the following:

1. __IR__   Interchangeable response to meaning: "You feel _____
   because _____."

2. __PM__   Personalized meaning: "You feel _____
   because you _____."

3. __PP__   Personalized problem: "You feel _____
   because you cannot _____."

4. __PG__   Personalized goal: "You feel_____
   because you cannot _____
   and you want to _____."

Example

| 28-Year-Old Woman: | "All my life, I've felt like I was searching for something. I know I'm a good person, I'm decent. I should be satisfied with who I am. But there's a sense of something missing. I'm not who I could be...I'm not strong or not complete somehow." |

__IR__   1. You feel dissatisfied because your life is not meeting your expectations.

__PM__   2. You feel angry with yourself because you have lost so much time.

__PM__   3. You feel sad because you might have lived your life differently if you'd had this missing information.

__PP__   4. You feel weak inside because you cannot define what is missing.

__PG__   5. You feel disappointed because you haven't yet determined what it is that is missing in your life and you want, deeply, to find it.

Exercise

1. **High School Girl:**   "It's really good talking to you like this. Usually, I can't talk with people my age, I'm self-conscious and uneasy. I feel really out of it—like I don't belong. I'm different from most young people...it's...well...I'd love to be social and relaxed. But I know I'm not one of them; they all stay away from me."

_____ a. You feel sad because people aren't friendly with you.

_____ b. You feel alone because people your age never welcome you as a friend.

_____ c. You feel unhappy because you have not made any friends.

_____ d. You feel alone because you cannot get along with people your age.

_____ e. You feel disappointed in yourself because you cannot relate to people your age and you want to be able to relate to them.

2. **Politician:**   "My whole life has been this way. Every time I get an opportunity to do something I seem to ruin it. I make terrible decisions, do dumb things, lose my temper...It's like I get scared and...deliberately ruin my chances."

_____ a. You feel angry because you destroy your opportunities.

_____ b. You feel frustrated because you blew your opportunities.

_____ c. You feel disgusted with yourself because you act impulsively and can-not act constructively.

_____ d. You feel depressed because your life has not been successful.

_____ e. You feel angry at yourself because you cannot control your actions and you want to be able to control your impulsive behavior.

3.	Professional Woman:	"My husband and I have always fought. Sometimes I think it's him...he's kind of a 'mama's boy'—his family always takes precedence. I don't know if I should have ever gotten married. I just seem to be...unhappy. And I work with so many attractive men. I get torn, conflicted. Why can't I settle down with the man I have?"

_____	a.	You feel confused because you cannot control your wandering eye.

_____	b.	You feel confused because you cannot make up your mind about how you feel and you want to settle this internal conflict.

_____	c.	You feel frustrated because you keep looking for something... somebody...who's more than your husband.

_____	d.	You feel angry at yourself because you cannot make a commitment to your husband.

_____	e.	You feel cheated because your husband never outgrew his childhood priorities.

4.	Mother:	"I don't want to fight with my kids all the time. I know that I'm responsible for giving them direction and helping them make wise decisions, but it is such a battle. Sometimes I feel like giving up."

_____	a.	You feel discouraged because raising kids is such a struggle.

_____	b.	You feel anxious because you don't want to fail them.

_____	c.	You feel disappointed with yourself because you don't always give your kids the constructive direction that they need.

_____	d.	You feel stuck because you can't relate to your kids without it turning into an argument and you want your communication with them to be positive, not a confrontation.

_____	e.	You feel exhausted because you can't keep up with your kids.

EXERCISE 45: PRACTICING PERSONALIZING GOALS

Introduction

In this exercise you will practice writing responses that personalize problems and goals.

Remember, a good personalized goal is really the flip-side of the problem and does not introduce a new behavior.

Instructions

Write a personalized problem and personalized goal response for each of the following statements.

Example

Woman: "God, I feel so damn guilty. I was sober for 18 months and I thought I had it all together. Then the tension got to me and I just fell apart."

1. Personalize the problem: <u>You feel discouraged with yourself because you can't handle the tension without the booze.</u>

2. Personalize the goal: <u>You feel discouraged because you can't handle stress without drinking and you want to learn constructive ways of dealing with stress.</u>

Exercise

1. 35-Year-Old Woman: "Oh, that bastard! He was beating me up so I divorced him, then had to get a restraining order to keep him away. He left me alone 'till he heard I had a new boyfriend and was putting my life back together. As soon as he heard that, he came back and beat up my boyfriend."

   a. Personalize the problem: You feel _____

   because you cannot _____

   b. Personalize the goal: You feel _____

   because you cannot _____

   _____ and you want to _____

   _____

109

2. Parent: "We tried so hard with him. We knew he had lots of problems so we tried to make it easy for him. I guess we were too easy when he was growing up. He has just taken and taken and taken from us. We've got to get him out of the house, for our own sanity."

a. Personalize the problem: You feel _____

because you cannot _____

b. Personalize the goal: You feel _____

because you cannot _____

_____ and you want to _____

_____

3. 33-Year-Old Woman: "I don't know quite how to say this but...uh...whenever..uh.... my husband wants to...go to bed with me, I just feel sick... I feel disgusted. I have to grit my teeth and think of the kid's welfare...If I don't...uh...sleep with him he'll leave me."

a. Personalize the problem: You feel _____

because you cannot _____

b. Personalize the goal: You feel _____

because you cannot _____

_____ and you want to _____

_____

4. Father: "I'm so worried about my daughter. She's had three nervous breakdowns in two years. Her husband's an alcoholic, beats her...I'm just sick. She refuses to leave him and she's getting worse and worse."

a. Personalize the problem: You feel _____

because you cannot _____

b. Personalize the goal: You feel _____

because you cannot _____

_____ and you want to _____

_____

EXERCISE 46: PRACTICING PERSONALIZING FEELINGS

Introduction

When helpees communicate how they feel about their problems they usually note a disappointment in themselves. When helpees communicate how they feel about their goals they usually note some optimism, as they can now see a way out of their problems. It is essential that helpers stay tuned to the helpee's changing feelings.

Instructions

Read the following helpee excerpts and then write a personalized response to feeling. Be sure to stay tuned to the helpees' feelings about their problems and goals.

Example

Young Woman: "You're so...together. I look at you and say, 'How does she do it?' You're not much older. But when I compare myself...I still live at home; I depend on my folks for everything. I feel like a kid next to you."

Personalized Feeling (about problem): You feel <u>disappointed with yourself</u> because <u>you can't live independently</u>.

Young Woman: "...yeah I get it. So if I just put this plan into effect, within 6 months I could have my own car and I would be a lot more independent!"

Personalized Feeling (about goal): You feel <u>excited now</u> because you <u>see that you can take charge of your own movement toward independence</u>.

Exercise

1a. Middle-Aged Man: "The doctors say it's my fault for not taking my medicine. But I forget. And the stuff makes me feel so tired. I know it's the only way to get rid of the infection but I forget. I get busy and I miss the time I'm supposed to take it."

Personalized Feeling (about problem): You feel _____

because you _____

111

1b. Middle-Aged Man: "I appreciate your lending me that alarm clock wristwatch. Now I'll be reminded when I need to take the medication. I'll be rid of this infection soon and back in the full swing of things again."

Personalized Feeling (about goal): You feel _____

because you _____

2a. Young Man: "I just can't stop eating! I can't set goals! I can't control myself!"

Personalized Feeling (about problem): You feel _____

because you _____

2b. Young Man: "I feel pretty good about myself right now because I know what I have to do to take control. I know I can take the weight off."

Personalized Feeling (about goal): You feel _____

because you _____

3a. Teenager: "I'd like to stop smoking dope but it's hard to do by myself. A lot of my friends smoke. How can I say 'No!'? I just don't know if I can say it."

Personalized Feeling (about problem): You feel _____

because you _____

3b. Teenager: "I see, so if I respond to my friends before I say 'No!', I show them that I respect them, and that sets them up to respect me and my decision not to smoke dope with them."

Personalized Feeling (about goal): You feel _____

because you _____

PERSONALIZING DECISION MAKING

Overview

We use decision-making strategies when we want to select from among alternatives. Decision making involves five major steps.

Step 1—Problem

We begin decision making by describing a personalized problem. We are able to describe a problem because we have been attentive to the situation and the people involved. We have observed and listened. And, we have responded interchangeably to check our understanding. We have communicated our understanding of what the situation means with a personalized response to meaning. Building upon this understanding, we are now able to formulate a response that describes the personalized problem. One way to describe personal problems is to describe them as skill, knowledge, or attitude deficits.

Example:

You feel directionless because you cannot decide which job opportunities to pursue.

Step 2—Goal

Next, we describe the personalized goal. One way to describe a personal goal is to describe the skill, knowledge, or attitude that would solve the problem or deficit.

Example:

You feel confused because you cannot decide which job opportunities to pursue and you want to pursue the job that will be best for you.

Step 3—Course of Action

Now, we may generate alternative courses of action. We may expand people options—"Who else might become involved?" We may expand program options—"What else might be done?" Or, we may expand organization options—"How else could we relate people and program options?"

Example:

- Publishing Company—Assistant Editor for a small company
- Consulting Company—Production work on projects
- Self-employment—Independent sub-contractor

Step 4—Values

We select our alternatives by using our values. Values are the meanings we attach to people, data, and things. Values are who and what matters to us. One helpful way of describing values is to describe the living, learning, and working benefits we wish to attain. We may now list the benefits we hope to gain. (It is understood that there are no benefits without some associated costs. When we define our values or the benefits we hope to gain, we will also include information about associated costs.)

Example:

Values

- Working Benefits — opportunity for advancement
- Learning Benefits — training opportunities
- Living Benefits — finances (salary) and commute, travel time

Step 5—Choices

Finally, we list our values and courses of action. We use our values to evaluate the courses of action. We evaluate how each course impacts each value. A helpful way of evaluating courses is to use the signs plus (+), minus (-), or neutral (0) to represent our estimations of how well or how poorly each alternative course will satisfy each value. After making this evaluation, we calculate the best alternative(s).

Example:

Courses of Action

Values	Publishing Co.	Consulting Co.	Self-employment
Advancement	+	0	0
Finances	+	+	0
Training	+	0	-
Commute	0	-	+

EXERCISE 47: USING DECISION-MAKING SKILLS

Introduction

Now you may practice these decision-making skills with a problem and goal of your own.

Instructions

Follow these five decision-making steps to determine the best solution for your problem.

Exercise

Step 1. Define a personalized problem.

I feel _____

because I cannot _____

Step 2. Define a personalized goal.

I feel _____

because I cannot _____

and I want to _____

Step 3. Now expand your possible courses of action. (Be sure to expand people, programs, and organization of resources.)

People	Programs	Organization of Resources
_____	_____	_____
_____	_____	_____
_____	_____	_____

Step 4. *List your values or the benefits you hope to gain. For example, these may be living, learning, or working benefits. (Also consider costs associated with these benfits.)*

Values

_____

_____

_____

_____

_____

Step 5. *Evaluate your alternative courses of action by estimating how well each course will satisfy each value. Now review your assessments to find the best choice or choices among your alternatives.*

For a more thorough study of decision making, see *Productive Problem-Solving,* R.R. Carkhuff, 1985, Amherst, MA: Human Resource Development Press.

EXERCISE 48: PERSONALIZING—COMMUNICATION

Introduction

This exercise is designed to help you master personalizing as a *systematic* process progressing from responses to meaning to personalizing goals.

Instructions

On the following pages are statements made by three people engaged in extensive exploration. After you read each statement, write your best response.

Exercise

1. Mother

a. "My children are starting to get out of hand. They've gotten so they don't listen to me or my husband unless we threaten them. And who wants to always have to threaten their children?"

Response to meaning: _____

_____

_____

b. "It's very frustrating. The oldest boy, Jimmy, was really well-behaved until this last year and then suddenly, it's like he's a different kid. He's wild now, always yelling and screaming. And last week I caught him twisting his brother's arm. I mean, he wanted to *hurt* him!"

Response to meaning: _____

_____

_____

c. "We're not a violent family—I don't know where he gets it from. I could maybe see it if I hit the kids all the time. But I don't. Oh, a swat now and then, but I never hurt them. Jimmy's getting mean, though—the kind of kid that's a bully."

Response to meaning: _____

_____

_____

d.   "It scares me really. You read stories about children who do really awful things. Jimmy isn't that bad, but it could happen."

Response to meaning: _____

_____

_____

e.   "Oh, I guess I'm not really that worried. He's a good kid actually. He can be very loving and cuddly. And sometimes he really cooperates. It's just that I want to be sure to catch this before it's out of my control. I love my son. And I don't want him growing up as some lonely bully. He can have a better life than that!"

Response to meaning: _____

_____

_____

f.   "That's really it, I guess. He's always been an introverted kid. Jimmy always seems to be alone. I used to ignore it. Try to tell myself he'd get more social as he got older. He seems so shy and...kinda sad... when he's in a group. My husband says, 'Leave the boy alone, he'll grow out of it.' But it breaks my heart, watching him always alone. And I know how much he wants to be part of it, to have others welcome him."

Response to meaning: _____

_____

_____

g.   "I guess I pressure him too much sometimes."

Response to personalized meaning: _____

_____

_____

h. "I'm really only trying to help. I don't get mad at him about it, not usually anyway. But I try to encourage him, give him ideas on how to get along. And lately, it's just backfiring. The more I press, the worse he seems to do...or he gets mean."

Response to personalized meaning: _____

_____

_____

i. "He's getting frustrated, too. And I do feel helpless. I've seen this developing and I just don't seem to be handling it. His brother models after him, too. I know that he needs something from me. What can I do?"

Response to personalized meaning: _____

_____

_____

j. "I've never had any trouble making friends. And I've always been comfortable with people. I was never the 'star', but I got along and I was happy."

Response to personalized meaning: _____

_____

_____

k. "I wish I could help Jimmy learn to do the same. I know it's what he needs—to feel good when he's with other children."

Response to personalized meaning: _____

_____

_____

l. "I just feel so bad. It seems like nothing I do works. I want to be a good mother...and I know this is a chance to really help my son. What if I fail?"

Response to personalized feeling and problem: _____

_____

_____

m. "I've tried before y'know. And look what happened...he started bullying the other kids. I know I shouldn't pressure him but it's important—for Jimmy. Someone's got to help him learn to get along with other kids, to be comfortable. And I'm his mother!"

Response to personalized feeling, problem, and goal: _____

_____

_____

2. **Young Man**

a. "Nothing is going right for me anymore. I quit my job last week and now I'm broke."

Response to meaning: _____

_____

_____

b. "Yeah, and I don't have any friends and my car's quit running again."

Response to meaning: _____

_____

_____

c. "My whole life has been this way. It seems like no matter what I try, I fail. Things just don't work for me."

Response to meaning: _____

_____

_____

d. "That's it. I'm miserable. The people I know all think I'm weird...different somehow. And it messes up everything for me. On my job, at home, when I was in school, it was like being in outer space. I can't relate to people and they all think I'm strange."

Response to meaning: _____

_____

_____

e. "I just feel so...so out of it. Like nothing I've ever done has made a difference. My life has been a waste. I do have a girlfriend now...whom I love. But sometimes I think she'd be better off without me."

Response to meaning: _____

_____

_____

f. "My touch is bad y'know. There's evil in me somehow and when I try to control it, it just busts out anyway. I don't want to hurt this girl, I love her."

Response to meaning: _____

_____

_____

g. "I'm alone, except for her. And if I ruined it with her, too...I know I could do it, too. I'm so...it's like being...y'know those horror movies you see. Where the foul monster consumes a beautiful girl. I know that's what'll happen if I let it."

Response to personalized meaning: _____

_____

_____

h. "I'll kill myself first...before I destroy her. She's the only thing good that ever touched my life."

Response to personalized meaning: _____

_____

_____

i. "I guess that's it. I just wanted to tell someone first."

Response to personalized meaning: _____

_____

_____

j.   "It's the right thing to do...kill myself. I'm miserable anyway. I might as well leave her happy. It'll be the only decent thing I've ever done."

Response to personalized meaning: _____

_____

_____

k.   "I can't keep living like this. I mean, if this is it...I'm better off dead."

Response to personalized feeling and problem: _____

_____

_____

l.   "I can't stand who I am...If I thought there was a chance...not for me... but for her, that maybe I could keep from hurting her...then...I don't really want to die. I'd like to be a real person to her, but I'll fail, I know it."

Response to personalized feeling, problem, and goal: _____

_____

_____

3. Ex-Convict

a.   "I've been looking hard but they don't give you a fair break. Once they know you've got that prison record they judge the record, not the man. They leave no room for people who have changed."

Response to meaning: _____

_____

_____

b.   "I feel trapped! Sure, I made mistakes when I was younger...what I did was wrong. But if I can't get a job, I'll have no choice. If I have to rob to feed myself, I'll rob!"

Response to meaning: _____

_____

_____

c. "Oh, I could do other things. Such crappy jobs though. You can't make a living pumping gas or sweeping stores. But that's all they'll let me have. I'm bad, y'know...can't be trusted, an ex-con. Makes me sick!"

Response to meaning: _____

_____

_____

d. "All the 'good' people turn up their noses. Employers look at me like I'm kidding when I apply for jobs. They don't want me."

Response to meaning: _____

_____

_____

e. "Y'know, when I was in prison I went through that new career training program—learned bookkeeping, some accounting, and even some computer skills. And years ago I did some work as a salesman—good at it too. What difference does it make though? Hell! With my clothes I even look like an ex-con! And after five minutes of side looks from those interviewers, I start to feel and act like what they think of me."

Response to meaning: _____

_____

_____

f. "There's just no room for me in that world."

Response to meaning: _____

_____

_____

g. "I'd be a good employee, too. I've got a lot to prove...to myself. It's time I learned to handle the world. I know I'd work hard and do what they asked as best I could...if I could just get that first job."

Response to personalized meaning: _____

_____

_____

h. "I always blow it though. They start to question me about my record and I just clam up. I know that makes 'em suspicious, too. Like if I can't talk about it, I must still be a crook. And they don't want an employee who acts like that. They've got enough problems."

Response to meaning: _____

_____

_____

i. "If only I could learn how to handle 'em when they come on about my record."

Response to personalized feeling and problem: _____

_____

_____

j. "I always feel so bad by the time I'm done. I've been enough of a loser."

Response to personalized meaning: _____

_____

_____

k. "I guess I'm so vulnerable to the way they think. I start to feel like I'm being judged and I just sink right into it. I don't project myself, I just act the way I think they're seeing me. I never seem to keep on—I give up."

Response to meaning: _____

_____

_____

l. "If I could just learn to remember that I've got things to offer, to contribute. Just because I've been to jail doesn't mean I'm through. I never do remember though. I blow it during the interview."

Response to personalized feeling and problem: _____

_____

_____

m. "I've got to learn to keep my cool, to handle these people and their ex-con questions. I want to get back in the job market. I want to be proud of who I am again."

Response to personalized feeling, problem, and goal: _____

_____

_____

EXERCISE 49: PERSONALIZING WITH YOURSELF

Introduction

You can use your personalizing skills to help understand your own problems too. In the following exercises you will help yourself to take control of your experience.

Instructions

Follow the instructions within each of the sections, then write responses to yourself.

Exercise

1. a.   Go back to Exercise 34 in this workbook and read one of the statements you wrote.

   b.   Write a new interchangeable response to yourself.

   I feel _____ because _____

   _____

   _____

   c.   Think about (explore) the situation further and write another response to yourself.

   I feel _____ because _____

   _____

   _____

   d.   Now, repeat Step c and write two more interchangeable responses to yourself.

   I feel _____ because _____

   _____

   _____

   I feel _____ because _____

   _____

   _____

e. Write a personalized meaning response to yourself for the same situation.

I feel _____ because I _____

_____

_____

f. Write another personalized meaning response to yourself for the same situation.

I feel _____ because I _____

_____

_____

g. Write a personalized problem response to yourself for the same situation.

I feel _____ because I cannot _____

_____

_____

h. Write a personalized goal response to yourself for the same situation.

I feel _____ because I cannot _____

_____

_____

and I want to _____

_____

2. a. Briefly describe another situation or experience which is important

to you. _____

_____

_____

_____

_____

b. Write a series of six interchangeable responses to yourself. After you
write each response, be sure to take time to *explore* how you feel
about the experience, and why.

I feel _____ because _____

_____

_____

I feel _____ because _____

_____

_____

I feel _____ because _____

_____

_____

I feel _____ because _____

_____

_____

I feel _____ because _____

_____

_____

I feel _____ because _____

_____

_____

c. Write a personalized meaning response to yourself .

I feel _____ because I _____

_____

_____

d.   Write another personalized meaning response to yourself.

I feel _____ because I _____

_____

_____

e.   Write a personalized problem response to yourself.

I feel _____ because I cannot _____

_____

_____

f.   Write a personalized goal response to yourself.

I feel _____ because I cannot _____

_____

and I want to _____

_____

EXERCISE 50: VIDEO EXERCISE—PERSONALIZING SKILLS

Introduction

This exercise will give you an opportunity to write some personalized responses—to meaning, problem, goal and feeling.

Instructions

Read the following questions then view the videotape *"Personalizing Skills."* Attend, observe and listen closely. The two graduate students present their problems to Dr. Carkhuff and he responds to them with several personalized responses. After viewing the videotape, write personalized responses to the graduate students. These are responses that you might have made if you had been the helper at the video-taping.

1. How did the graduate students feel when they began the video session? And why did they feel that way? Write a personalized response to meaning.

   You feel _____ because you _____

   _____

2. What was their problem? Write a personalized response to the problem.

   You feel _____ because you cannot ____

   _____

3. Now respond to their goal.

   You feel _____ because you cannot ____

   _____

   and you want to _____

4. When the graduate students found out that they could reach their goal, their outlook changed. Respond to this new feeling by personalizing the feeling.

   You feel _____ because you _____

   _____

5. INITIATING—FACILITATING HELPEE ACTING

OVERVIEW

You have learned to attend and respond to another person's experience. You have learned to personalize the person's understanding of the experience. The final helpee goal is *acting* to change or improve the experience. You will need *initiating skills* in order to facilitate action.

Initiating involves defining the goal, developing the steps to the goal, determining a schedule for completing the steps and for reinforcing the achievement of the goal. An example of initiating is given below, followed by exercises which are designed to help you learn to initiate with another person.

Before you complete the exercises in this chapter, read pages 181–213 in *The Art of Helping.*

Example

Personalized Goal:

You feel helpless inside because you cannot respond in a helpful way to your children and you want to learn to respond to them.

Operationalized Goal:

You want to respond to your children by building an interchangeable base of communication as indicated by the number of interchangeable responses you make to them at home.

Steps to the Goal:

1. Arrange room to attend contextually.
   a. Arrange furniture without barriers.
   b. Eliminate distractions.

2. Attend posturally
   a. Square
   b. Lean
   c. Make eye contact

3. Respond to content
   a. Listen to 5WH (who, what, when, where, why, and how)
   b. Recall
   c. Communicate: "You said _____"

4. Respond to feeling
   a. Ask yourself, "How would I feel if I were that person?"
   b. Select category and intensity
   c. Communicate: "You feel _____"

5. Respond to meaning
   a. Recall main theme
   b. Identify feeling and reason for the feeling
   c. Communicate: "You feel _____ because _____"

Schedule:

STEPS	START	FINISH
1. Attend Contextually	February 8	February 8
2. Attend Posturally	February 9	Continue through program
3. Respond to Content	February 10	February 15
4. Respond to Feeling	February 16	February 21
5. Respond to Meaning (Feeling and Content)	February 22	Continue indefinitely; check: February 28

Reinforcements:

Positive: $30 for new shoes

Negative: No one helps me with dinner dishes

EXERCISE 51: EXPLORING INITIATING SKILLS

Introduction

This exercise will help you understand your personal experiences with initiating.

Instructions

Answer each of the following questions.

Exercise

1. Describe a goal that you have successfully achieved.

   _____

   _____

2. Why do you think you were able to reach your goal? What did <u>you</u> do that made it possible?

   _____

   _____

   _____

   _____

   _____

   _____

3. Describe a goal that you failed to achieve.

   _____

   _____

4. Why did you fail? What is it that <u>you</u> did or did not do that resulted in your failure?

   _____

   _____

   _____

   _____

   _____

   _____

DEFINING GOALS

OVERVIEW

An operationalized goal is a goal that is defined in terms that are observable and measurable. We define goals so that the helpee will know when he or she has reached them.

Before doing the next three exercises, review the section on defining the goal in *The Art of Helping*, pages 186–189.

EXERCISE 52: DISCRIMINATING HELPEE BEHAVIORS IN OPERATIONALIZED GOALS

Introduction

The operational definition of the goal should be stated as behaviors that are controlable by the helpee. This exercise will help you learn to identify when an operational goal includes helpee behaviors.

Instructions

In the following operationalized goals, identify whether the goal is stated in terms of *helpee* behavior or *someone else's* behavior.

Example

Personalized goal:

You feel disgusted with yourself because you cannot respond constructively to your wife and you want to be able to respond.

a. You want to be able to respond constructively to your wife as indicated by the number of times you make a response to meaning with her at home.

☑ Helpee Behavior ☐ Not a Helpee Behavior

b. You want to be able to respond to your wife as indicated by how often she gets mad at you.

☐ Helpee Behavior ☑ Not a Helpee Behavior

Exercise

1. Personalized goal:

   You feel angry because you can't concentrate on your reading and you want to learn to concentrate.

   a. You want to learn to concentrate as indicated by the number of books and articles that you finish reading.

   ☐ Helpee Behavior   ☐ Not a Helpee Behavior

   b. You want to learn to concentrate as indicated by the number of important points you can recall, and put into writing, at the end of each time period.

   ☐ Helpee Behavior   ☐ Not a Helpee Behavior

   c. You want to learn to concentrate as indicated by the number of people who interrupt you while you are trying to read.

   ☐ Helpee Behavior   ☐ Not a Helpee Behavior

2. Personalized goal:

   You feel angry with yourself because you can't stop doing too many "extras" for your ex-husband and you want to be able to stop.

   a. You want to stop doing inappropriate extras as indicated by the number of new things he demands of you.

   ☐ Helpee Behavior   ☐ Not a Helpee Behavior

   b. You want to stop doing inappropriate extras as indicated by saying "no" to some of his demands.

   ☐ Helpee Behavior   ☐ Not a Helpee Behavior

   c. You want to stop doing inappropriate extras as indicated by the number of times you turn down a demand for something he doesn't deserve.

   ☐ Helpee Behavior   ☐ Not a Helpee Behavior

3. Personalized goal:

You feel worried because you can't remember to take your medication regularly and you want to be able to remember.

a. You want to remember to take your medication as indicated by the number of days a week that you actually take it.

☐ Helpee Behavior   ☐ Not a Helpee Behavior

b. You want to remember to take your medication as indicated by the number of times the doctor reprimands you.

☐ Helpee Behavior   ☐ Not a Helpee Behavior

c. You want to remember to take your medication as indicated by taking your pills.

☐ Helpee Behavior   ☐ Not a Helpee Behavior

EXERCISE 53: DISCRIMINATING MEASURABLE GOALS

Introduction

An operationalized goal deals with the helpee's behavior *and* is measurable. An operationalized goal is measurable when the behavior is stated in terms of a quantity (number of, percent of, amount of time).

Instructions

Now, go back to Exercise 52 and circle the goals that are both helpee behaviors and are *measurable* behaviors.

Example

Personalized goal:

> You feel disgusted with yourself because you cannot respond constructively to your wife and you want to be able to respond.

(1.) You want to be able to respond constructively to your wife as indicated by the number of times you make a response to meaning with her at home.

    ☑ Helpee Behavior   ☐ Not a Helpee Behavior

2. You want to be able to respond to your wife as indicated by how often she gets mad at you.

    ☐ Helpee Behavior   ☑ Not a Helpee Behavior

EXERCISE 54: PRACTICING DEFINING GOALS

Introduction

This exercise will help you learn to write operational goals. An operational goal is defined by the following interrogatives.

- Who or *what* is involved in the goal?

- What will the people and/or things involved do?

- How and *why* will it be done?

- Where and *when* will it be done?

- How well will it be performed so the helpee will know when the goal is achieved?

Next, we must communicate our definition of the goal to the helpee in these operational terms. We do this by emphasizing observable and measurable behaviors and standards of performance. Standards are usually described in terms of the number of times or the amount of time the helpee will perform some behavior.

Instructions

For each of the following situations, make the goal operational by using the 5WH interrogatives. After you complete the interrogatives, write a statement that communicates this goal to the helpee, stating what will be done (behavior) and how it will be done (standards of performance).

Example

a. Personalized goal:

> You feel disappointed because you can't relate effectively to your parents and you want to be able to.

b. Operationalized goal:

Who or what:	helpee and parents
What:	to relate effectively
How and Why:	by responding accurately to increase communication
When and Where:	at home during meal times
How Well:	lay an interchangeable base—at least 6 responses

c. Communicate the goal to the helpee:

>You want to <u>be able to relate effectively with your parents</u>
>
>(BEHAVIOR)
>
>as indicated by <u>the number of interchangeable responses you</u>
>
><u>make to them during meal times</u> (STANDARDS)

Exercise

1. Freshman girl (from a very small town) who is now at a large college and who refuses to leave her roommate's side.

   a. Personalized goal:

   >You feel lost because you don't know how to go about making new friends and you want to learn how to.

   b. Operationalized goal:

   >Who or What: _____
   >
   >What: _____
   >
   >How and Why: _____
   >
   >When and Where: _____
   >
   >How Well: _____

   c. Communicate the goal to the helpee:

   >You want to _____
   >
   >_____(BEHAVIOR)
   >
   >as indicated by _____
   >
   >_____(STANDARDS)

2. Man, early 30's, who has been complaining about his wife always nagging him, while he very frequently is the one to initiate the arguments.

   a. Personalized goal:

        You feel disappointed because you can't control your temper with your wife.

   b. Operationalized goal:

        Who or What: _____

        What: _____

        How and Why: _____

        When and Where: _____

        How Well: _____

   c. Communicate the goal to the helpee:

        You want to _____

        _____(BEHAVIOR)

        as indicated by _____

        _____(STANDARDS)

3. Businesswoman, passed over for position as manager of a department.

   a. Personalized goal:

        You feel trapped because you can't demonstrate any clear evidence of your managerial ability and you want to be able to prove your ability.

   b. Operationalized goal:

        Who or What: _____

        What: _____

        How and Why: _____

        When and Where: _____

        How Well: _____

   c. Communicate the goal to the helpee:

        You want to _____

        _____(BEHAVIOR)

        as indicated by _____

        _____(STANDARDS)

4. Young first-time offender having hassles with one prison guard who likes to threaten him.

   a. Personalized goal:

      You feel scared because you can't handle the guard's threats and you want to be able to.

   b. Operationalized goal:
      Who or What: _____
      What: _____
      How and Why: _____
      When and Where: _____
      How Well: _____

   c. Communicate the goal to the helpee:
      You want to _____

      _____(BEHAVIOR)

      as indicated by _____

      _____(STANDARDS)

5. Black man in staff position at a college feels the administrators go out of their way to create special positions for him but won't give him anything important—he's their token black.

   a. Personalized goal:

      You feel angry because you can't get the promotion on your merits and you want to make it because of who you are.

   b. Operationalized goal:
      Who or What: _____
      What: _____
      How and Why: _____
      When and Where: _____
      How Well: _____

   c. Communicate the goal to the helpee:
      You want to _____

      _____(BEHAVIOR)

      as indicated by _____

      _____(STANDARDS)

DEVELOPING PROGRAMS

OVERVIEW

Initiating steps to the goal means identifying and sequencing the first step, the intermediate steps, and the necessary sub-steps that the person must do in order to reach the goal.

Before completing these exercises, review the section on Developing Programs in *The Art of Helping*, pages 190–194.

EXERCISE 55: MAKING SURE THE STEPS TO A GOAL ARE BEHAVIORS

Introduction

Steps to the goal should be observable and measurable behaviors. A good step is specific and tells the person what he or she will do.

Instructions

Identify which of the steps below are observable and measurable behaviors. Check *yes* if the step is a behavior, and *no* if it is not a behavior.

Example

	BEHAVIOR	
	YES	**NO**
1. Try harder	☐	☑
2. Read one book	☑	☐
3. Attend posturally	☑	☐
4. Get in shape	☐	☑
5. Run 1/2 mile	☑	☐
6. Be more open	☐	☑

Exercise

		BEHAVIOR	
	YES		**NO**
1. Rewrite the essay	☐		☐
2. Ask two questions	☐		☐
3. Be curious	☐		☐
4. Act creative	☐		☐
5. Think fast	☐		☐
6. Recall 5WH	☐		☐
7. Personalize the meaning	☐		☐
8. Do 15 sit-ups	☐		☐
9. Write one 1,000 calorie diet	☐		☐
10. Eat less	☐		☐
11. Lose weight	☐		☐
12. Sit down without reading	☐		☐
13. Be empathic	☐		☐
14. Call Al-Anon two times daily	☐		☐
15. Feel more confident	☐		☐
16. Watch less television	☐		☐
17. Ignore it	☐		☐
18. Read the want ads	☐		☐
19. Plan ahead	☐		☐
20. Confront her	☐		☐
21. List two assets	☐		☐
22. Nourish him	☐		☐
23. Respond to her feelings	☐		☐
24. Don't get depressed	☐		☐
25. Spend 1/2 hour alone	☐		☐

EXERCISE 56: PRACTICING INITIATING STEPS

Introduction

The first step in developing steps to a goal is to brainstorm a list of the behaviors necessary to take a person to his or her goal.

Instructions

For each of the following people, brainstorm possible steps (behaviors) to lead them to accomplish their operationalized goal. You do not need to develop a step for each line given, only the steps you think are needed to achieve the goal. Remember that steps are "behaviors."

Example

Janine: Janine is a 24-year-old mother of two. Ashley is two-and-a-half years of age and is walking and climbing everywhere. Allison, the baby, is almost fourteen months old. She's up on her feet, too, and getting more mobile each day. They are happy babies with one exception. They both have terrible skin rashes and the rashes affect them emotionally. When their skin conditions are very dry and blotchy looking, they get very irritable. What is Janine to do?

Janine's first operationalized goal:
> I want to try some health initiatives that will minimize the severity of the children's rashes as indicated by a reduction in dry blotchy skin and by a reduction in irritable behaviors exhibited by the children.

Brainstorm some steps for Janine:

Keep a diary of what the children eat

Vacuum the rugs at the end of each day

Keep the dog out of the rooms where the children live

Invest in a quality air cleaner

Take the children to the doctor for a check-up

Get plastic covers for the children's matresses

Exercise

1. Sam:

Sam is an 18-year-old drug user—predominantly he uses alcohol although he also smokes marijuana, takes amphetamines, and has snorted cocaine. Sam came in complaining of feeling alone, abused, and disgusted with himself. He is in poor physical shape: standing 5'11" and weighing only 137 pounds. Sam graduated from high school last year with no vocational skills and only a C- average. He has few friends and considers the friends he has to be a negative influence. Sam is depressed and scared about his future.

Sam's first operationalized goal:

I want to quit taking alcohol and all other drugs as indicated by the number of days I am "straight" this month.

Brainstorm some steps for Sam:

_____

_____

_____

_____

_____

_____

_____

2. Rita: Rita is suffering from a severe bout with depression. She was a relatively happy person until 3 months ago when she caught her husband in bed with another woman. She has left her husband and is staying with her sister and her sister's husband. Rita finds that the littlest reminder of her estranged husband sets her off into fits of crying. She is both furious at him and full of pain. Rita has filed for divorce. She is feeling really down because at age 40, she is without a job and without hope. She is terrified that she will end up spending the rest of her life alone.

Rita's first operationalized goal:

I want to regain my self-worth and dignity as indicated by the number of days of word-processing work that I can get this month.

Brainstorm some steps for Rita:

_____

_____

_____

_____

_____

_____

_____

3. Mary: Mary is a 19-year-old who has developed a severe phobia about soap which interferes with her daily life. She refuses to bathe or wash her clothes or hair. Because Mary looks and smells unkempt, she is without friends and does not leave her parents' house. She is unable to gain and hold a job or go to school. Mary feels ashamed of herself because she cannot use soap without fear and she wants to use soap to bathe and care for herself.

Mary's first operationalized goal:

I want to be unafraid of soap as indicated by the percent of times I use soap to care for myself without feeling anxious afterwards.

Brainstorm some steps for Mary:

_____

_____

_____

_____

_____

_____

_____

EXERCISE 57: PRACTICING DEVELOPING SUB-STEPS

Introduction

This exercise will increase your ability to divide behaviors into smaller behaviors or sub-steps. Sub-steps increase the likelihood that the person will achieve a goal. Sub-steps should be observable and measurable behaviors which lead to a step in a program. Developing sub-steps is done by first brainstorming the behaviors necessary to accomplish a step and then sequencing these behaviors as sub-steps.

Instructions

On the following pages, use the steps that you brainstormed in Exercise 56 then develop appropriate sub-steps for each step. Use only as many steps and substeps as you feel are necessary.

Example

Operationalized goal:

I want to get in shape as indicated by the number of miles I run each week.

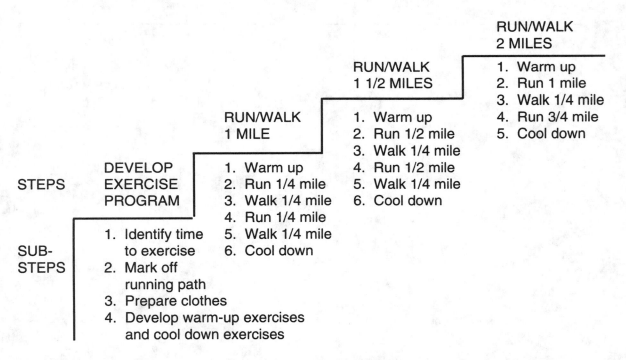

NOTE: The step ladder form used above and on the following pages is one way to represent an entire program. If you prefer, you may also write your program in the more familiar outline form as illustrated on the following page.

Operationalized goal:

I want to get in shape as indicated by the number of miles I run each week.

I. Develop Exercise Program

    1. Identify time to exercise
    2. Mark off running path
    3. Prepare clothes
    4. Develop warm-up exercises and cool-down exercises

II. Run/Walk 1 Mile

    1. Warm up
    2. Run 1/4 mile
    3. Walk 1/4 mile
    4. Run 1/4 mile
    5. Walk 1/4 mile
    6. Cool down

III. Run/Walk 1 and 1/2 Miles

    1. Warm up
    2. Run 1/2 mile
    3. Walk 1/4 mile
    4. Run 1/2 mile
    5. Walk 1/4 mile
    6. Cool down

IV. Run/Walk 2 Miles

    1. Warm up
    2. Run 1 mile
    3. Walk 1/4 mile
    4. Run 3/4 mile
    5. Cool down

Exercise

1. Sam: "I want to quit taking alcohol and all other drugs as indicated by the number of days I am 'straight' this month."

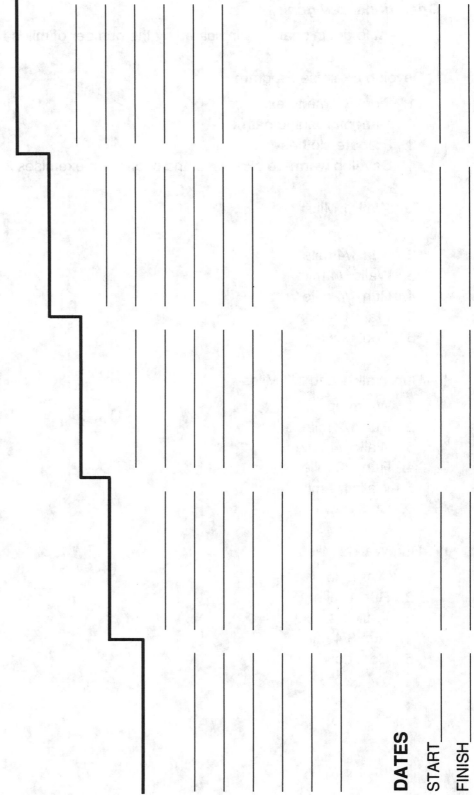

DATES

START _____

FINISH _____

150

Exercise

2. Rita: "I want to regain my self-worth and dignity as indicated by the number of days of word-processing work that I can get this month."

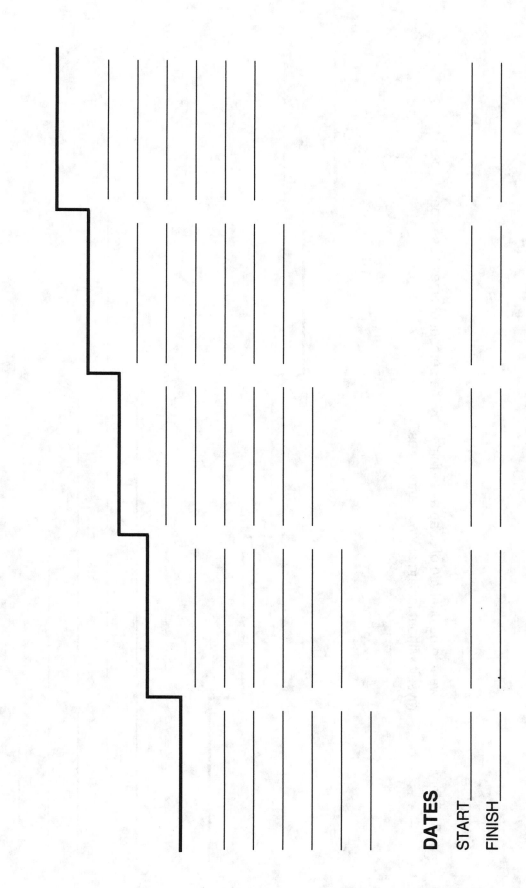

DATES

START _____

FINISH _____

Exercise

3. Mary: "I want to be unafraid of soap as indicated by the percent of times I use soap to care for myself without feeling anxious afterwards."

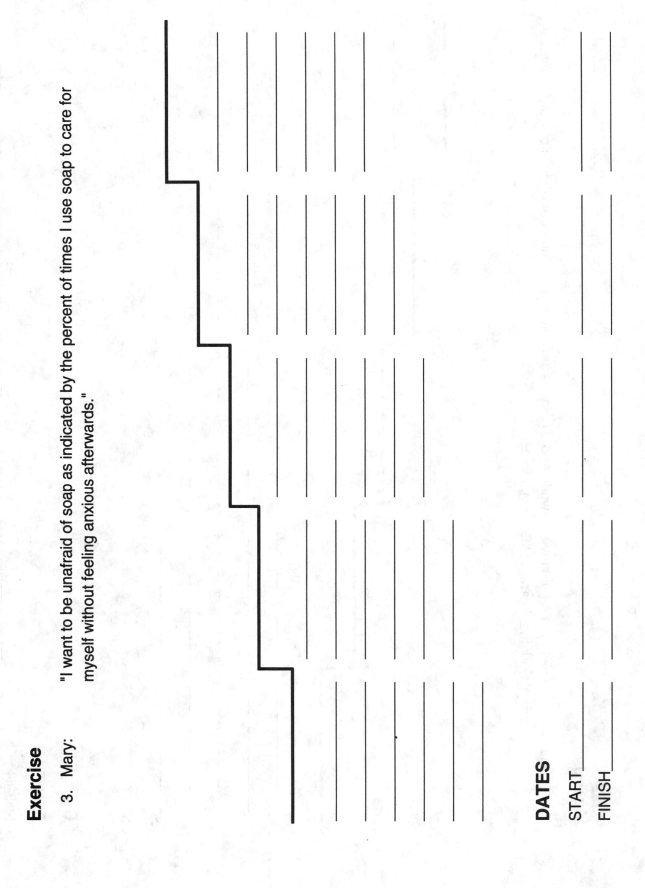

DATES

START _____

FINISH _____

152

DEVELOPING SCHEDULES

OVERVIEW

Scheduling means setting a starting date and a finishing date for each step (not sub-step) that the person must take to achieve the goal.

Review pages 195–198 in *The Art of Helping* before completing this section.

EXERCISE 58: PRACTICING DEVELOPING SCHEDULES

Instructions

Go back to the steps you copied for Exercise 57 and write start and finish dates for each step in two of the three programs. Use the lines provided at the bottom of each of those pages. Imagine that the helpee (Sam, Rita, Mary) is starting the program tomorrow.

DEVELOPING REINFORCEMENTS

OVERVIEW

Developing reinforcements encourages the helpee to take the needed steps by making the consequences of his/her actions immediate.

Review pages 199–202 on Developing Reinforcements in *The Art of Helping*.

EXERCISE 59: DISCRIMINATING TYPES OF REINFORCEMENTS

Introduction

This exercise will help you expand the repertoire of reinforcers you might use with any helpee.

When initiating a program, you can use two types of reinforcers. These are:

- Positive Reinforcers: adding a *desirable* consequence for completing a step in the program

- Negative Reinforcers: withholding something *desirable* or adding something *disliked* as a consequence for *not* completing a step in the program

Instructions

Indicate whether each item is a positive or negative reinforcer.

Example

	POSITIVE	NEGATIVE
1. Free trip to Acapulco	✓	
2. Not being able to wear a favorite suit		✓
3. Getting a spanking		✓
4. Not having to do the dishes	✓	

			POSITIVE	NEGATIVE
1.	a.	Buy a new CD	☐	☐
	b.	Not getting to play a favorite CD in the evening	☐	☐
	c.	Having to do math homework during a time I usually just listen to music	☐	☐
	d.	Playing music loud in the evening whenever I want	☐	☐
2.	a.	Being grounded	☐	☐
	b.	Having to baby-sit for a younger brother when grounded on Saturday night	☐	☐
	c.	Getting to stay out one hour later than usual	☐	☐
	d.	Not going to a movie with friends	☐	☐
3.	a.	Earning an "A" on a paper	☐	☐
	b.	Losing the right to socialize during study hall	☐	☐
	c.	Getting permission to go on a field trip	☐	☐
	d.	Completing an extra written assignment if paper is late	☐	☐
4.	a.	Doing the dishes for an extra week	☐	☐
	b.	Having someone else cook for the week	☐	☐
	c.	Having to wash the pots and pans in addition to the other dishes	☐	☐
	d.	No television after supper	☐	☐
5.	a.	Getting a hot fudge sundae	☐	☐
	b.	Not getting a hot fudge sundae	☐	☐
	c.	Losing a normally eaten dessert	☐	☐
	d.	No supper	☐	☐

EXERCISE 60: PRACTICING INITIATING REINFORCEMENTS

Introduction

This exercise will help you expand the reinforcers you employ for yourself and others.

Instructions

Develop a positive reinforcer and negative reinforcer for each person you wrote a program for in Exercise 57. Remember to keep the reinforcements appropriate for the goal and to make them fit the person's frame of reference.

Example

Alice: "I want to earn more freedom at home as indicated by the number of times each week I make my own decisions about where I go, after which my parents approve of what I did."

a. Positive reinforcer: <u>Normal weekly allowance of $15.00 to be spent on entertainment if Alice completes step.</u>

b. Negative reinforcer: <u>Normal weekly allowance of $15.00 put in savings account if Alice fails to complete step.</u>

Exercise

1. Sam: "I want to quit taking alcohol and all other drugs as indicated by the number of days I am 'straight' this month."

a. Positive reinforcer: _____

_____

b. Negative reinforcer: _____

_____

2. Rita: "I want to regain my self-worth and dignity as indicated by the number of days of word-processing work that I can get this month."

   a. Positive reinforcer: _____

     _____

   b. Negative reinforcer: _____

     _____

3. Mary: "I want to be unafraid of soap as indicated by the percent of times I use soap to care for myself without feeling anxious afterwards."

   a. Positive reinforcer: _____

     _____

   b. Negative reinforcer: _____

     _____

EXERCISE 61: VIDEO EXERCISE—INITIATING SKILLS

Introduction

This exercise will give you an opportunity to initiate a program.

Instructions

Read the following exercise then view the videotape *"Initiating Skills."* Now initiate a program for the graduate students on the videotape.

Exercise

1. Write a personalized response to the graduate students' goal of learning helping skills.

   You feel _____ because you cannot

   and you want to _____.

2. Now operationalize the graduate students' goal.

   You want to _____

   (BEHAVIOR)

   as indicated by _____

   (STANDARDS)

3. Initiate steps to the operationalized goal.

BRAINSTORM STEPS	SEQUENCE
_____	_____
_____	_____
_____	_____
_____	_____
_____	_____
_____	_____

4. Add sub-steps and outline these steps and sub-steps.

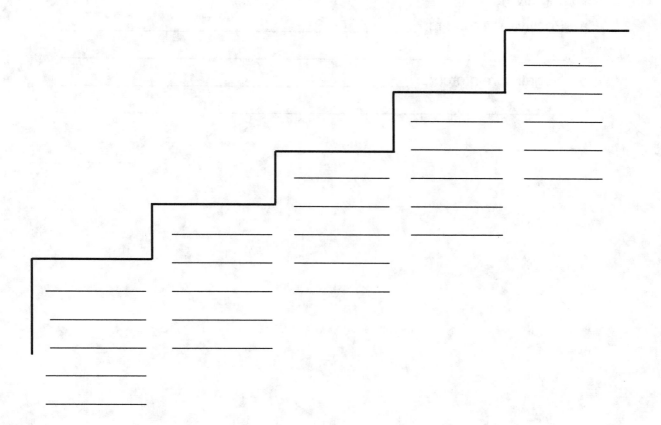

5. Initiate a potential schedule.

STEP	START	FINISH
_____	____	____
_____	____	____
_____	____	____
_____	____	____

6. Suggest some potential reinforcements for the students (list two positive and two negative).

    a. Positive reinforcers: _____

    _____

    b. Negative reinforcers: _____

    _____

IMPLEMENTING STEPS

EXERCISE 62: PRACTICING INITIATING

Introduction

This exercise will help you rehearse all the steps of initiating.

Instructions

Peter has come to you for help. You have attended to Peter, responding to his exploration, and personalized Peter's goal. Now you must initiate to help Peter act. In initiating with Peter you will operationalize his goal, develop steps to the goal and sub-steps for each step, and initiate a schedule and reinforcements.

Example

Review examples from Exercises 51–61 as needed.

Exercise

Background:

Peter is a 25-year-old man who has been living in the community for one year. His family lives 3,000 miles away although he does have a distant cousin, 15 years older than he, in the city where he now lives. He sees the cousin perhaps once a month when he visits him for supper. Although he is college educated (English major), Peter is presently unemployed. He eats poorly because of his financial status and does little exercise. Peter has very few friends and spends the largest percentage of his time alone in his apartment, reading. The majority of his reading deals with depressing subject matters.

Peter sought your help because for the past two months he has been hearing voices. He is scared because his mother once had him hospitalized for "craziness." He is depressed because his life is lonely and empty. You and Peter have personalized his goal and feeling as "You feel afraid of yourself, Peter, because you cannot stop the voices and you want to stop the voices before you become 'crazy' again."

1. Operationalize Peter's goal (5WH Behavior and Standards).

   You want to _____

   as indicated by _____

   _____

2. Initiate steps to Peter's operationalized goal.

BRAINSTORM STEPS	SEQUENCE
_____	_____
_____	_____
_____	_____
_____	_____
_____	_____
_____	_____

3. Add sub-steps to Peter's outline of steps:

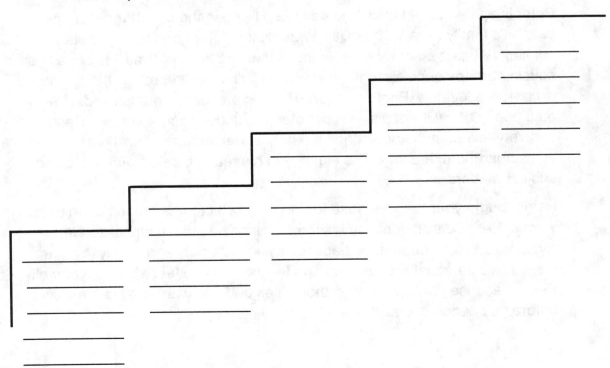

162

4. Initiate a schedule for Peter.

STEP	START	FINISH
_____	_____	_____
_____	_____	_____
_____	_____	_____
_____	_____	_____
_____	_____	_____

5. Initiate reinforcements for Peter (list two positive and two negative).

    a. Positive reinforcers: _____

             _____

    b. Negative reinforcers: _____

             _____

EXERCISE 63: INITIATING WITH YOURSELF

Introduction

You are ready to initiate with your own experience using the steps you learned for initiating with others. Turn back to Exercise 49 and review the base of interchangeable responses and personalized responses you wrote to yourself.

Instructions

Write personalized responses and a program for yourself including goals, steps, schedule, and rewards. Follow the directions given at each point.

Exercise

1. Review your personalized goal.

   I feel _____

   because I cannot _____

   and I want to _____

2. Operationalize your goal.

   I want to _____

   as indicated by _____

   _____

3. Initiate steps to your operationalized goal.

BRAINSTORM STEPS	SEQUENCE
_____	_____
_____	_____
_____	_____
_____	_____
_____	_____
_____	_____

4. Add sub-steps to your outline of steps.

_____

_____
_____
_____
_____

_____   _____
_____   _____
_____   _____

_____   _____   _____
_____   _____   _____
_____   _____   _____

5. Initiate a schedule for yourself.

STEP	START	FINISH
_____	_____	_____
	_____	_____
	_____	_____
	_____	_____
	_____	_____

6. Initiate reinforcements for yourself (list two positive and two negative).

   a. Positive reinforcers: _____

_____

   b. Negative reinforcers: _____

_____

EXERCISE 64: REVIEWING PROGRAM STEPS

OVERVIEW

Implementation steps enable us to implement our programs. They include reviewing, rehearsing, and revising the steps.

Introduction

Reviewing is the first implementation step and involves reviewing all of the steps in the program. It gives us a chance to make sure that we have included all the necessary steps.

Instructions

Refer back to your program in Exercise 63 of this workbook. Review the definition of your goal, steps of your program, time schedule, and reinforcements. Indicate any changes that you make in the space provided.

Your review _____

_____

_____

_____

_____

_____

EXERCISE 65: REHEARSING PROGRAM STEPS

Introduction

This exercise will help you practice the next step of program implementation—rehearsing the steps. Rehearsing involves practicing the skill in a controlled setting before attempting the program steps in the intended setting. Rehearsal increases the probability of achieving the goal.

Instructions

Read the following situations and indicate how the helpees could rehearse the skills before attempting their actual goals.

Example

A young man defines his goal as wanting to communicate effectively with his wife, as indicated by responding to her feelings and content.

He could rehearse the steps to his goal by: <u>practicing his responding</u> <u>skills within a classroom setting to ensure mastering the skills before</u> <u>attempting his goal.</u>

Exercise

1. A young woman wants to be honest with her boyfriend as indicated by the amount of time she spends telling him her true feelings.

   She could rehearse the steps to her goal by: _____

   _____

   _____

   _____

   _____

2. A factory worker wants a higher salary as indicated by his ability to ask his boss for a raise.

He could rehearse the steps to his goal by: _____

_____

_____

_____

_____

3. An alcoholic wants to face her drinking problem as indicated by her ability to state to her family that she is an alcoholic.

She could rehearse the steps to her goal by: _____

_____

_____

_____

_____

EXERCISE 66: REVISING PROGRAM STEPS OR GOALS

Introduction

Revising is the third implementation step. When we act on our programs we get feedback which will indicate if we need to revise any steps or goals in our programs.

Instructions

Read the following helpee situations and revise the programs based on the feedback given.

Example

A woman's goal is to run 3 miles in 25 minutes within 6 weeks. In the fourth week of her program she realizes the goal is unrealistic.

A possible revision could be <u>instead of running 3 miles in 25 minutes</u> <u>she will revise the time to 30 minutes.</u>

Exercise

1. A college student's goal is to read one new novel a week but he realizes that he does not have enough time to do this.

   A possible revision could be _____

   _____

2. A young executive has begun managing three projects but learns that his skills in management are poor. He does not want the projects to fail.

   A possible revision could be _____

   _____

3. A doctor puts his patient on a 1,000-calorie-per-day diet. After one week of this, the feedback indicates that his patient cannot stick to this diet because the patient does not know how to count calories.

   A possible revision could be _____

   _____

PLANNING CHECK STEPS

OVERVIEW

We can build success into our programs by developing before, during, and after check steps. Check steps emphasize the physical, emotional, and intellectual resources we need to complete each step. Review pages 207–210 in *The Art of Helping* for more information on Planning Check Steps.

EXERCISE 67: PLANNING CHECK STEPS

Introduction

This exercise will enable you to develop detailed programs so that you ensure the success of your goals. Check steps emphasize the things we need to think about before, during, and after the performance of each step. "Before Check Steps" ask and answer the question: "What resources will I need to be able to perform the step successfully?" "During Check Steps" ask and answer the question: "Am I performing the step correctly?" "After Check Steps" ask and answer the question: "Did I achieve the results and get the benefits I wanted?"

Instructions

Read the following programs. For each of the steps, fill in some appropriate before, during, and after check step questions.

Example

A 40-year-old woman states her goal:

"I want to get in shape as indicated by the number of miles I can run-walk."

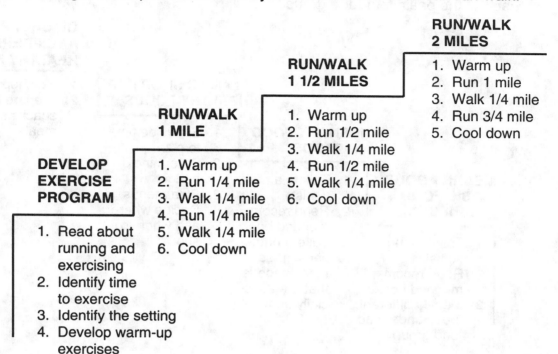

**RUN/WALK
2 MILES**

1. Warm up
2. Run 1 mile
3. Walk 1/4 mile
4. Run 3/4 mile
5. Cool down

**RUN/WALK
1 1/2 MILES**

1. Warm up
2. Run 1/2 mile
3. Walk 1/4 mile
4. Run 1/2 mile
5. Walk 1/4 mile
6. Cool down

**RUN/WALK
1 MILE**

1. Warm up
2. Run 1/4 mile
3. Walk 1/4 mile
4. Run 1/4 mile
5. Walk 1/4 mile
6. Cool down

**DEVELOP
EXERCISE
PROGRAM**

1. Read about running and exercising
2. Identify time to exercise
3. Identify the setting
4. Develop warm-up exercises

BEFORE:	BEFORE:	BEFORE:	BEFORE:
Do I have the distance measured? Do I have a stop watch? Do I have good running shoes?	Do I have my equipment?	How do I feel about running?	Do I like my equipment? Do I like my route?
DURING:	**DURING:**	**DURING:**	**DURING:**
Does what I read make sense?	Am I performing all of the stretching exercises that I need to?	Is my motivation still strong?	How hard am I breathing? What is my heart rate?
AFTER:	**AFTER:**	**AFTER:**	**AFTER:**
Do I know what to do? Did I start properly?	Did I cover the distance? What was my time?	Do I feel more relaxed? Is it getting easier?	What was my time? Do I feel healthier now?

Exercise

1. A 28-year-old expectant mother states her goal:

   "I want to eat healthier as indicated by the number of calories that I eat under each of the basic four food groups."

GO SHOPPING AND PREPARE HEALTHY FOODS

1. Go shopping
2. Prepare healthy snacks and meals

PLAN TO SHOP FOR HEALTHY FOODS

1. Set aside time to plan
2. Determine budget
3. Plan menus
4. Decide where and when to shop

IDENTIFY FOOD HAZARDS

1. Talk to a nutritionist
2. Read recommended books
3. Take a nutrition course
4. Identify foods that are especially unhealthy

LEARN ABOUT BASIC FOOD GROUPS

1. Talk to a nutritionist
2. Read recommended books
3. Identify different foods under each food group

BEFORE:	**BEFORE:**	**BEFORE:**	**BEFORE:**
DURING:	**DURING:**	**DURING:**	**DURING:**
AFTER:	**AFTER:**	**AFTER:**	**AFTER:**

2. 20-year-old son states his goal:

"I want to develop a better relationship with my father as indicated by the number of conversations I initiate with him about myself."

INITIATE CONVERSATION

1. Attend, observe, and listen to him
2. Talk about something important
3. Ask for his advice or thoughts

ENGAGE FATHER

1. Tell him I am looking forward to eating with him
2. Check the time with him

SCHEDULE MEAL TIMES

1. Find out the exact times for meals
2. Plan my schedule each week

IDENTIFY CONVERSATION TOPICS

1. Identify topics important to me
2. Identify topics he may be able to relate to
3. Identify topics he might be able to give me advice on

BEFORE:	BEFORE:	BEFORE:	BEFORE:
DURING:	DURING:	DURING:	DURING:
AFTER:	AFTER:	AFTER:	AFTER:

3 Summary

6. RECYCLING THE HELPING PROCESS

OVERVIEW

You have now learned and practiced a complete cycle of helping skills. You can use these skills with yourself and others to solve problems and achieve goals in living, learning, and working environments.

EXERCISE 68: USING ALL OF YOUR HELPING SKILLS

Introduction

You have practiced each of the skills of helping: attending, responding, personalizing, and initiating. You can now help another person to explore, understand, and act.

In the following exercise, you are asked to use all of your helping skills when writing your most effective responses and initiatives to the person "speaking."

Instructions

Make your best response to each excerpt, following the response format listed below it.

Exercise

Social Caseworker

1. "He's a very disturbed young man. Listen to him when he talks. His voice is full of depression. Sounds very crazy to me."

   Response to meaning: _____

   _____

   _____

2. "Well...he's so manipulative. That's what gets to me when I work with him. Just the things he says. It's evident that he's trying to get the world revolving around him—operating on his schedule. It gets to me. I want to tell him to grow up, the world isn't waiting for him."

   Response to meaning: _____

   _____

   _____

177

3. "Last week he came in and saw me. Boy—did he ever dump on me! He's gotten himself suspended from school for fighting, his mother was threatening to throw him out of the house, and he'd found this job-corps program he says I should get him into. So I try to help, and I must've spent eight hours scrambling for him, but I just don't have that kind of time. He's not my only client."

Response to meaning: _____

_____

_____

4. "I just feel like he's not trying at all. He wants to lay back and be this 'poor me' and have everybody else provide for him."

Response to meaning: _____

_____

_____

5. "You can't help people who won't work for themselves. He's got to take action himself!"

Response to meaning: _____

_____

_____

6. "I find it very draining to work with him. Sometimes after he leaves I just sit and think, 'What am I doing this for?' There are no rewards, just a lot of discouragement. I care about him—about all my clients."

Response to personalized meaning: _____

_____

_____

7. "It seems like I care about them more than they care about themselves. It takes a piece of me every time I watch one of my clients mess up."

Response to personalized meaning: _____

_____

_____

8. "I get so sad...and tired. I feel like I'm one of society's garbage and trash recyclers. And I'm fighting and scratching and trying to save what's good. And the 'garbage' itself keeps fighting me."

Response to personalized meaning: _____

_____

_____

9. "What is it? How do I stop it? I want to get through to these people...to this sad, lonely young man. And I'm not."

Response to personalized problem: _____

_____

_____

10. "You know, I took this job because I love people. Want to help them. And here I am, starting to hate my clients—and myself. I can't help them; I fail so many of my clients."

Response to personalized problem: _____

_____

_____

11. "Here I am, bitter and defeated, I can't help them. Yet, I'm it—I'm their only chance. If I quit, if we all quit, it'd be worse. I want to help still, but not like this...pouring my guts and my clients' down these bottomless holes. There has to be an alternative."

Response to personalized goal: _____

_____

_____

12. Operationalize this person's goal.

_____

_____

_____

_____

_____

13. Initiate steps to this person's operationalized goal (use the chart on the following page).

14. Initiate sub-steps leading to each step (use the chart on the following page).

15. Initiate a schedule.

STEP	START	FINISH
_____	_____	_____
_____	_____	_____
_____	_____	_____
_____	_____	_____
_____	_____	_____

16. Initiate reinforcements:

   a. Positive reinforcers: _____

      _____

   b. Negative reinforcers: _____

      _____

Operationalized Goal: _____

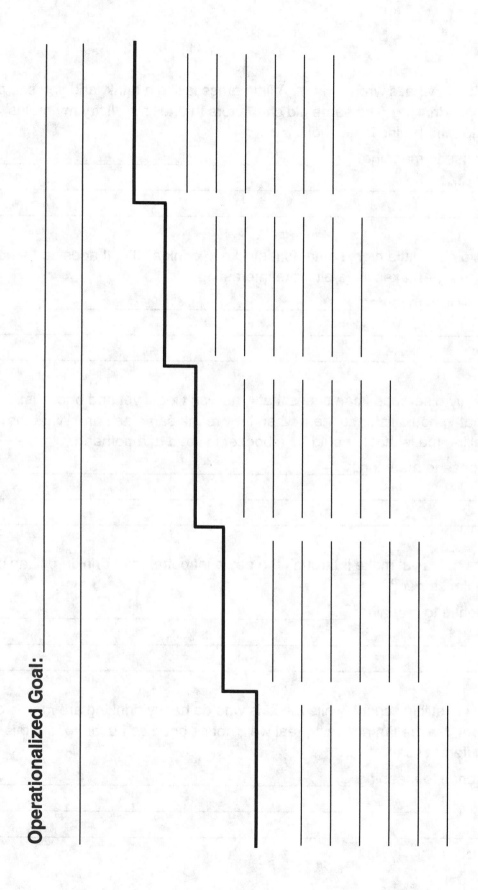

Teenager

1. "I don't see what's wrong with it. A little grass is like a drink, and you see plenty of people drinking. The same old characters that tell me I'll 'fry my brains' are soaking their brains in alcohol."

   Response to meaning: _____

   _____

   _____

2. "I like to get a little high, same as they like to drink a little. It adds up to the same thing—makes life a bit more interesting."

   Response to meaning: _____

   _____

   _____

3. "The only difference I can see is that grass isn't legal yet and booze is. They say that I should listen to them when they're the same as I am. What they're really telling me is that I should be a boozer instead of a pothead."

   Response to meaning: _____

   _____

   _____

4. "Grass helps ya' make it through the day a lot better than drinking. I can do OK when I'm stoned."

   Response to meaning: _____

   _____

   _____

5. "Like, I'm still in school, while the kids who do heavy drinking are mostly on the way out. Maybe I'm not doing real well, not as good as I used to, but this school is a different scene."

   Response to meaning: _____

   _____

   _____

6. "Sometimes getting high is the only way to stand it here. The teachers want all this work done, and I was never super-smart and all the kids are phoney here, except for those who smoke."

Response to meaning: _____

_____

_____

7. "Every time I turn around someone's putting pressure on me—do this, change that. If I'm high, everything's cool."

Response to personalized meaning: _____

_____

_____

8. "Grass is all right. When I'm with my friends it doesn't matter if I'm living up to their expectations. I know who I am then and I'm OK."

Response to personalized meaning: _____

_____

_____

9. "Yeah, it does bug me that people don't see who I am, that they can't accept me as a person, with or without the grass. Grass does give me some people who accept me—somehow I just can't get the others to see who I am."

Response to personalized problem: _____

_____

_____

10. "I like me...I want others to. I used to be able to make it, before I came to this school. I guess that's when I started smoking all the time..."

Response to personalized goal: _____

_____

_____

11. Operationalize this person's goal:

_____

_____

_____

_____

_____

12. Initiate steps to this person's operationalized goal (use the chart on the next page).

13. Initiate sub-steps leading to each step (use the chart on the next page).

14. Initiate a schedule.

STEP	START	FINISH
_____	_____	_____
_____	_____	_____
_____	_____	_____
_____	_____	_____
_____	_____	_____

15. Initiate reinforcements:

   a. Positive reinforcers: _____

_____

   b. Negative reinforcers: _____

_____

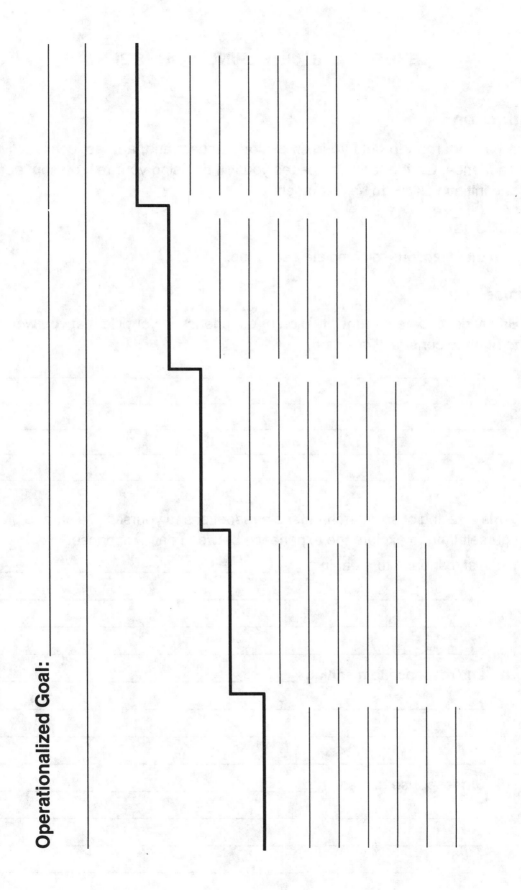

Operationalized Goal:

EXERCISE 69: HELPING YOURSELF

Introduction

You have learned to help yourself explore, understand, and act constructively on your experience. On the following pages you will be using your responding, personalizing, and initiating skills to help yourself.

Instructions

Follow the directions to complete each step.

Exercise

1. Briefly describe a current situation or experience in your life that you would like to bring to constructive action.

   _____

   _____

   _____

   _____

   _____

2. Write a series of six interchangeable responses to yourself. Be sure to give yourself time to explore the experience between each response.

   a. *1st* response to meaning: _____

   _____

   _____

   _____

   b. *2nd* response to meaning: _____

   _____

   _____

   _____

   c. *3rd* response to meaning: _____

   _____

   _____

   _____

d. *4th* response to meaning: _____

_____

_____

_____

e. *5th* response to meaning: _____

_____

_____

_____

f. *6th* response to meaning: _____

_____

_____

_____

3. Personalize your experience. Be sure to take time to understand before pro-
ceeding to the next response.

   a. Response to personalized meaning: _____

_____

_____

_____

   b. Response to personalized meaning: _____

_____

_____

_____

   c. Response to personalized problem: _____

_____

_____

_____

   d. Response to personalized goal: _____

_____

_____

_____

4. Initiate to help yourself act on your personalized experience.

   Your operationalized goal: _____

   _____

   _____

   _____

   _____

   _____

5. Brainstorm steps leading towards your operationalized goal:

   _____

   _____

   _____

   _____

   _____

   _____

   _____

   _____

   _____

   _____

   _____

6. Use the chart on the next page to record and sequence the steps to your goal.
   Also add appropriate sub-steps for each goal.

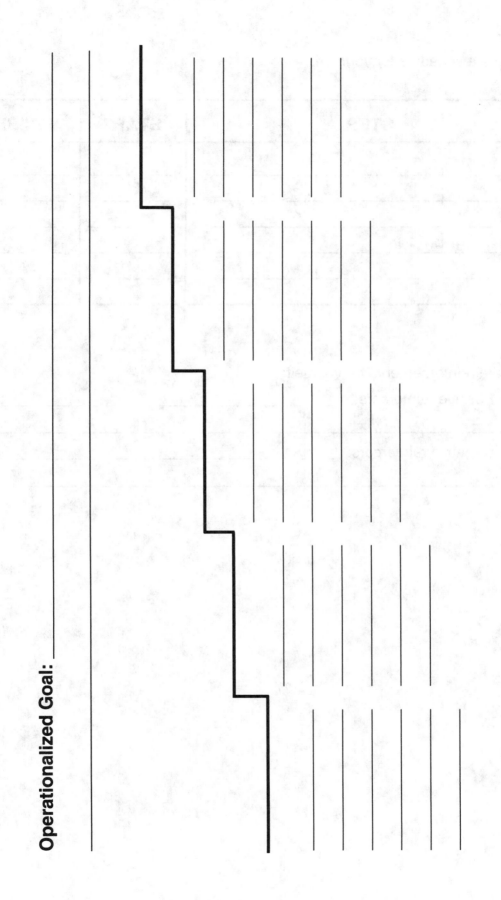

Operationalized Goal: _____

7. Initiate a schedule for yourself.

STEP	START	FINISH
_____	_____	_____
_____	_____	_____
_____	_____	_____
_____	_____	_____
_____	_____	_____

8. Initiate reinforcements for yourself:

   a. Positive reinforcers: _____

   _____

   b. Negative reinforcers: _____

   _____

EXERCISE 70: VIDEO EXERCISE—HELPING GIL

Introduction

The real challenge of helping occurs in the helping process. During a counseling session the helping process is recycled. Effective helpers facilitate extensive exploration, accurate understanding and effective acting by the helpee.

Instructions

To complete this exercise you will need access to the videotape "Helping Gil." Before viewing the video read through the following questions and directions. (This exercise can be used as a large group experience or can be completed during and after a personal showing of the videotape.)

1. Begin by viewing the videotape and by focusing your observation skills. After a few minutes stop the video and record your observations and inferences about Gil on the following chart.

APPEARANCE	BEHAVIOR	INFERENCE
Posture:	*Body Movements:*	*Energy Level:* High – Medium – Low
Facial Expressions:		*Feelings:* Up – Mixed – Down
Grooming:		
Body Build:		*Congruence:* High – Medium – Low
Sex:		
Age:		
Race:		

2. As you watch the video, make a list of the feelings that Gil is experiencing. You will see that as he moves through exploration, understanding and action, his feelings change. You will also notice that Dr. Carkhuff stays tuned to these changing feelings.

_____   _____

_____   _____

_____   _____

_____   _____

_____   _____

_____   _____

_____   _____

_____   _____

_____   _____

3. Watch and listen to the entire helping session. Dr. Carkhuff uses the skills of helping to facilitate Gil's movements through exploration, understanding and action. Re-create the helping session with you as the helper. Follow these directions.

Respond interchangeably (feeling and content) to Gil as he presents himself early in the counseling session. Use the initial feeling words you listed as a basis for your responses.

3a. You feel _____ because _____

_____

3b. You feel _____ because _____

_____

3c. You feel _____ because _____

_____

4. Now personalize the meaning for Gil.

You feel _____ because you _____

_____

5. Write a personalized response to communicate Gil's problem.

    You feel _____ because you cannot _____

    _____

6. Communicate how Gil feels about his deficit.

    You feel _____ because _____

    _____

7. What is Gil's goal? Communicate the personalized goal.

    You feel _____ because you cannot _____

    _____ and you want to

    _____

8. How does Gil feel about the asset he wishes to have (his goal)?

    You feel _____ because _____

    _____

9. Next, operationalize the goal for Gil. Do this by describing the first step in operational terms.

    Who or What is involved?   _____

    What will be done?   _____

    How and Why will it be done?   _____

    When and Where will it be done?   _____

    How Well will it be done?   _____

10. Use this space to brainstorm some further steps that Gil might take to reach his goal.

    _____

    _____

    _____

    _____

    _____

EXERCISE 71: VIDEO EXERCISE — HELPING COLLEEN

Introduction

The real challenge of helping occurs in the helping process. During a counseling session the helping process is recycled. Effective helpers facilitate extensive exploration, accurate understanding and effective acting by the helpee.

Instructions

To complete this exercise you will need access to the videotape *"Helping Colleen."* Before viewing the video read through the following questions and directions. (This exercise can be used as a large group experience or can be completed during and after a personal showing of the videotape.)

1. Begin by viewing the videotape and by focusing your observation skills. After a few minutes stop the video and record your observations and inferences about Colleen on the following chart.

APPEARANCE	BEHAVIOR	INFERENCE
Posture: *Facial Expressions:* *Grooming:* *Body Build:* *Sex:* *Age:* *Race:*	*Body Movements:*	*Energy Level:* High – Medium – Low *Feelings:* Up – Mixed – Down *Congruence:* High – Medium – Low

2. As you watch the video, make a list of the feelings that Colleen is experiencing. You will see that as she moves through exploration, understanding and action, her feelings change. Also note that Dr. Carkhuff stays tuned to these changing feelings.

_____   _____
_____   _____
_____   _____
_____   _____
_____   _____
_____   _____
_____   _____
_____   _____
_____   _____

3. Watch and listen to the entire helping session. Dr. Carkhuff uses the skills of helping to facilitate Colleen's movements through exploration, understanding and action. Re-create the helping session with you as the helper. Follow these directions.

Respond interchangeably (feeling and content) to Colleen as she presents herself early in the counseling session. Use the initial feeling words you listed as a basis for your responses.

3a. You feel _____ because _____
     _____

3b. You feel _____ because _____
     _____

3c. You feel _____ because _____
     _____

4. Now personalize the meaning for Colleen.

You feel _____ because you _____
_____

5. Write a personalized response to communicate Colleen's problem.

   You feel _____ because you cannot _____

   _____

6. Communicate how Colleen feels about her deficit.

   You feel _____ because _____

   _____

7. What is Colleen's goal? Communicate the personalized goal.

   You feel _____ because you cannot _____

   _____ and you want to

   _____

8. How does Colleen feel about the asset she wishes to have (her goal)?

   You feel _____ because _____

   _____

9. Next, operationalize the goal for Colleen. Do this by describing the first step in operational terms.

   Who or What is involved?   _____

   What will be done?   _____

   How and Why will it be done?   _____

   When and Where will it be done?   _____

   How Well will it be done?   _____

10. Use this space to brainstorm some further steps that Colleen might take to reach her goal.

    _____

    _____

    _____

    _____

    _____

EXERCISE 72: VIDEO EXERCISE—HELPING TYRONE

Introduction

The real challenge of helping occurs in the helping process. During a counseling session the helping process is recycled. Effective helpers facilitate extensive exploration, accurate understanding and effective acting by the helpee.

Instructions

To complete this exercise you will need access to the videotape *"Helping Tyrone."* Before viewing the video read through the following questions and directions. (This exercise can be used as a large group experience or can be completed during and after a personal showing of the videotape.)

1. Begin by viewing the videotape and by focusing your observation skills. After a few minutes stop the video and record your observations and inferences about Tyrone on the following chart.

APPEARANCE	BEHAVIOR	INFERENCE
Posture:	*Body Movements:*	*Energy Level:* High – Medium – Low
Facial Expressions:		*Feelings:* Up – Mixed – Down
Grooming:		
Body Build:		*Congruence:* High – Medium – Low
Sex:		
Age:		
Race:		

2. As you watch the video, make a list of the feelings that Tyrone is experiencing. You will see that as he moves through exploration, understanding and action, his feelings change. Also note that Dr. Carkhuff stays tuned to these changing feelings.

      _____   _____

      _____   _____

      _____   _____

      _____   _____

      _____   _____

      _____   _____

      _____   _____

      _____   _____

3. Watch and listen to the entire helping session. Dr. Carkhuff uses the skills of helping to facilitate Tyrone's movements through exploration, understanding and action. Re-create the helping session with you as the helper. Follow these directions.

Respond interchangeably (feeling and content) to Tyrone as he presents himself early in the counseling session. Use the initial feeling words you listed as a basis for your responses.

    3a.   You feel _____ because _____

            _____

    3b.   You feel _____ because _____

            _____

    3c.   You feel _____ because _____

            _____

4. Now personalize the meaning for Tyrone.

    You feel _____ because you _____

    _____

5. Write a personalized response to communicate Tyrone's problem.

   You feel _____ because you cannot _____

   _____

6. Communicate how Tyrone feels about his deficit.

   You feel _____ because _____

   _____

7. What is Tyrone's goal? Communicate the personalized goal.

   You feel _____ because you cannot _____

   _____ and you want to

   _____

8. How does Tyrone feel about the asset he wishes to have (his goal)?

   You feel _____ because _____

   _____

9. Next, operationalize the goal for Tyrone. Do this by describing the first step in operational terms.

   Who or What is involved?   _____

   What will be done?   _____

   How and Why will it be done?   _____

   When and Where will it be done?   _____

   How Well will it be done?   _____

10. Use this space to brainstorm some further steps that Tyrone might take to reach his goal.

    _____

    _____

    _____

    _____

    _____

EXERCISE 73: VIDEO EXERCISE—HELPING ROSE

Introduction

The real challenge of helping occurs in the helping process. During a counseling session the helping process is recycled. Effective helpers facilitate extensive exploration, accurate understanding and effective acting by the helpee.

Instructions

To complete this exercise you will need access to the videotape *"Helping Rose."* Before viewing the video read through the following questions and directions. (This exercise can be used as a large group experience or can be completed during and after a personal showing of the videotape.)

1. Begin by viewing the videotape and by focusing your observation skills. After a few minutes stop the video and record your observations and inferences about Rose on the following chart.

APPEARANCE	BEHAVIOR	INFERENCE
Posture:	*Body Movements:*	*Energy Level:* High – Medium – Low
Facial Expressions:		
		Feelings: Up – Mixed – Down
Grooming:		
Body Build:		*Congruence:* High – Medium – Low
Sex:		
Age:		
Race:		

2. As you watch the video, make a list of the feelings that Rose is experiencing. You will see that as she moves through exploration, understanding and action, her feelings change. Also note that Dr. Berenson stays tuned to these changing feelings.

_____   _____

_____   _____

_____   _____

_____   _____

_____   _____

_____   _____

_____   _____

_____   _____

_____   _____

3. Watch and listen to the entire helping session. Dr. Berenson uses the skills of helping to facilitate Rose's movements through exploration, understanding and action. Re-create the helping session with you as the helper. Follow these directions.

Respond interchangeably (feeling and content) to Rose as she presents herself early in the counseling session. Use the initial feeling words you listed as a basis for your responses.

3a. You feel _____ because _____

_____

3b. You feel _____ because _____

_____

3c. You feel _____ because _____

_____

4. Now personalize the meaning for Rose.

You feel _____ because you _____

_____

5. Write a personalized response to communicate Rose's problem.

   You feel _____ because you cannot _____

   _____

6. Communicate how Rose feels about her deficit.

   You feel _____ because _____

   _____

7. What is Rose's goal? Communicate the personalized goal.

   You feel _____ because you cannot _____

   _____and you want to

   _____

8. How does Rose feel about the asset she wishes to have (her goal)?

   You feel _____ because _____

   _____

9. Next, operationalize the goal for Rose. Do this by describing the first step in operational terms.

   Who or What is involved?   _____

   What will be done?   _____

   How and Why will it be done?   _____

   When and Where will it be done?   _____

   How Well will it be done?   _____

10. Use this space to brainstorm some further steps that Rose might take to reach her goal.

    _____

    _____

    _____

    _____

    _____

EXERCISE 74: VIDEO EXERCISE—A CONVERSATION WITH GODWIN

Introduction

The real challenge of helping occurs in the helping process. During a counseling session the helping process is recycled. Effective helpers facilitate extensive exploration, accurate understanding and effective acting by the helpee.

Instructions

To complete this exercise you will need access to the videotape "A Conversation with Godwin." Before viewing the video read through the following questions and directions. (This exercise can be used as a large group experience or can be completed during and after a personal showing of the videotape.)

1. Begin by viewing the videotape and by focusing your observation skills. After a few minutes stop the video and record your observations and inferences about Godwin on the following chart.

APPEARANCE	BEHAVIOR	INFERENCE
Posture:	*Body Movements:*	*Energy Level:* High – Medium – Low
Facial Expressions:		*Feelings:* Up – Mixed – Down
Grooming:		
Body Build:		*Congruence:* High – Medium – Low
Sex:		
Age:		
Race:		

2. As you watch the video, make a list of the feelings that Godwin is experiencing. You will see that as he moves through exploration, understanding and action, his feelings change. You will also notice that Dr. Berenson stays tuned to these changing feelings.

_____   _____

_____   _____

_____   _____

_____   _____

_____   _____

_____   _____

_____   _____

_____   _____

_____   _____

3. Watch and listen to the entire helping session. Dr. Berenson uses the skills of helping to facilitate Godwin's movements through exploration, understanding and action. Re-create the helping session with you as the helper. Follow these directions.

   Respond interchangeably (feeling and content) to Godwin as he presents himself early in the counseling session. Use the initial feeling words you listed as a basis for your responses.

   3a.   You feel _____ because _____

         _____

   3b.   You feel _____ because _____

         _____

   3c.   You feel _____ because _____

         _____

4. Now personalize the meaning for Godwin.

   You feel _____ because you _____

   _____

5. Write a personalized response to communicate Godwin's problem.

 You feel _____ because you cannot _____

 _____

6. Communicate how Godwin feels about his deficit.

 You feel _____ because _____

 _____

7. What is Godwin's goal? Communicate the personalized goal.

 You feel _____ because you cannot _____

 _____ and you want to

 _____

8. How does Godwin feel about the asset he wishes to have (his goal)?

 You feel _____ because _____

 _____

9. Next, operationalize the goal for Godwin. Do this by describing the first step in operational terms.

 Who or What is involved? _____

 What will be done? _____

 How and Why will it be done? _____

 When and Where will it be done? _____

 How Well will it be done? _____

10. Use this space to brainstorm some further steps that Godwin might take to reach his goal.

 _____

 _____

 _____

 _____

 _____

EXERCISE 75: VIDEO EXERCISE—HELPING GEORGE

Introduction

The real challenge of helping occurs in the helping process. During a counseling session the helping process is recycled. Effective helpers facilitate extensive exploration, accurate understanding and effective acting by the helpee.

Instructions

To complete this exercise you will need access to the videotape "Helping George." Before viewing the video read through the following questions and directions. (This exercise can be used as a large group experience or can be completed during and after a personal showing of the videotape.)

1. Begin by viewing the videotape and by focusing your observation skills. After a few minutes stop the video and record your observations and inferences about George on the following chart.

APPEARANCE	BEHAVIOR	INFERENCE
Posture:	*Body Movements:*	*Energy Level:* High – Medium – Low
Facial Expressions:		*Feelings:* Up – Mixed – Down
Grooming:		
Body Build:		*Congruence:* High – Medium – Low
Sex:		
Age:		
Race:		

2. As you watch the video, make a list of the feelings that George is experiencing. You will see that as he moves through exploration, understanding and action, his feelings change. You will also notice that Dr. Carkhuff stays tuned to these changing feelings.

_____   _____

_____   _____

_____   _____

_____   _____

_____   _____

_____   _____

_____   _____

_____   _____

3. Watch and listen to the entire helping session. Dr. Carkhuff uses the skills of helping to facilitate George's movements through exploration, understanding and action. Re-create the helping session with you as the helper. Follow these directions.

Respond interchangeably (feeling and content) to George as he presents himself early in the counseling session. Use the initial feeling words you listed as a basis for your responses.

3a. You feel _____ because _____

_____

3b. You feel _____ because _____

_____

3c. You feel _____ because _____

_____

4. Now personalize the meaning for George.

You feel _____ because you _____

_____

5. Write a personalized response to communicate George's problem.

You feel _____ because you cannot _____

_____

6. Communicate how George feels about his deficit.

You feel _____ because _____

_____

7. What is George's goal? Communicate the personalized goal.

You feel _____ because you cannot _____

_____ and you want to

_____

8. How does George feel about the asset he wishes to have (his goal)?

You feel _____ because _____

_____

9. Next, operationalize the goal for George. Do this by describing the first step in operational terms.

Who or What is involved? _____

What will be done? _____

How and Why will it be done? _____

When and Where will it be done? _____

How Well will it be done? _____

10. Use this space to brainstorm some further steps that George might take to reach his goal.

_____

_____

_____

_____

_____

EXERCISE 77: VIDEO EXERCISE—HELPING YOUTH

Introduction

The real challenge of helping occurs in the helping process. During a counseling session the helping process is recycled. Effective helpers facilitate extensive exploration, accurate understanding and effective acting by the helpee.

Instructions

To complete this exercise you will need access to the videotape *"Helping Youth."* Before viewing the video read through the following questions and directions. (This exercise can be used as a large group experience or can be completed during and after a personal showing of the videotape.)

1. Begin by viewing the videotape and by focusing your observation skills. After a few minutes stop the video and record your observations and inferences about this group on the following chart.

APPEARANCE	BEHAVIOR	INFERENCE
Posture:	*Body Movements:*	*Energy Level:* High – Medium – Low
Facial Expressions:		
		Feelings: Up – Mixed – Down
Grooming:		
Body Build:		*Congruence:* High – Medium – Low
Sex:		
Age:		
Race:		

2. As you watch the video, make a list of the feelings that the youth are experiencing. Note that John stays tuned to their changing feelings.

_____   _____
_____   _____
_____   _____
_____   _____
_____   _____
_____   _____
_____   _____
_____   _____
_____   _____

3. Watch and listen to the entire helping session. John uses the skills of helping to facilitate the youths' movements through exploration, understanding and action. Re-create the helping session with you as the helper. Follow these directions.

Respond interchangeably (feeling and content) to these youth as they present themselves early in the group session. Use the feeling words that you listed above as a basis for your responses.

3a.   You feel _____ because _____

_____

3b.   You feel _____ because _____

_____

3c.   You feel _____ because _____

_____

4. Now write a personalized meaning to any one youth or to the group.

You feel _____ because you _____

_____

5. Write a personalized response to communicate either an individual's problem or the group's problem.

   You feel _____ because you cannot _____
   _____

6. Communicate how either an indiviudal youth or the group feels about their deficit(s).

   You feel _____ because _____
   _____

7. What is the goal of the group? Or, the goals of the individuals? Communicate a personalized goal.

   You feel _____ because you cannot _____
   _____ and you want to
   _____

8. How do any of the youth feel about the assets they wish to have (their goal)? Or how does the group feel about the assets they wish to have (their goal)?

   You feel _____ because _____
   _____

9. Next, operationalize the goal for any of the youth or for the group as a whole. Do this by describing a first step in operational terms.

   Who or What is involved?   _____

   What will be done?   _____

   How and Why will it be done?   _____

   When and Where will it be done?   _____

   How Well will it be done?   _____

10. Use this space to brainstorm some further steps that the youth might take to reach their goal(s).

   _____
   _____
   _____
   _____
   _____

POST-TEST

OVERVIEW

You have now practiced the basic skills of helping. At this point, you should review where you are in relation to these skills, both to see how far you have come and to begin to set new goals for yourself.

These two Post-tests will give you an opportunity to measure your ability to both *communicate* helpfully and to *discriminate* helpful responses. (Once you have completed both the communication and discrimination post-tests you may ask an expert (your teacher or trainer), to rate your communication post-test or you may refer back to the *Art of Helping* text to help you to rate your response yourself. You may turn to pages 216 and 217 of this workbook for answers to the discrimination post-test and to record your ratings.

A. POST-TEST: COMMUNICATING HELPING SKILLS

Instructions

Imagine the you have been interacting with the following helpee for about 20 minutes. The helpee, a young executive in a retail business, says to you:

"I don't know what's going on. I get good performance reviews, better than some people who've left, but I don't seem to be able to get promoted to the next level. I was reviewed six months ago, and I'm still waiting to move up. They say I'm doing excellent work, but one senior executive says I'm too aggressive and another says I'm not aggressive enough. I can't please everybody, yet it looks like I have to."

Write down what you would say to this helpee. Write the exact words you would use if you were actually speaking to the helpee.

_____

_____

_____

_____

_____

_____

B. POST-TEST: DISCRIMINATING HELPING SKILLS

Introduction

Throughout this workbook you have learned to discriminate and communicate accurate and effective responses. This post-test will help to review the accuracy of your discriminations.

Instructions

Imagine that a young executive in a retail business has been talking to a helper for about 20 minutes. This is an excerpt of what the executive has been saying:

"I don't know what's going on. I get good performance reviews, better than some people who've left, but I don't seem to be able to get promoted to the next level. I was reviewed six months ago, and I'm still waiting to move up. They say I'm doing excellent work, but one senior executive says I'm too aggressive and another says I'm not aggressive enough. I can't please everybody, yet it looks like I have to."

Following are several alternative responses that might have been made by someone trying to help this person. Next to each response, write a number to indicate your rating of the effectiveness of that response. Use the following scale:

1.0	=	Very Ineffective
2.0	=	Ineffective
3.0	=	Minimally Effective
4.0	=	Very Effective
5.0	=	Extremely Effective

_____ a. You don't know what to make of the situation, how to please both parties so you can get promoted.

_____ b. You feel frustrated because you can't reach the level you're capable of and you want to move up.

_____ c. The business world is like that sometimes. They'll keep you there as long as they can if you're doing a good job. Only pesonalities get promoted!

_____ d. You feel stuck because you're not sure what you have to do to prove you're capable of handling the next level and you want to get the promotion. You might begin by discussing with your bosses what *behaviors* they see as aggressive or nonaggressive, then working out a compromise with them.

_____ e. You're confused because your bosses give you contradictory messages.

213

PRE-TEST DISCRIMINATION SCORESHEET

To calculate your discrimination score, use the Pre-test Discrimination Scoresheet below and follow these steps:

1. Fill in your ratings for each of the five responses. These ratings indicate your ratings of the effectiveness of the five responses.

2. Without regard to whether the difference is positive or negative, write the difference between your ratings and the expert ratings. This will result in five "difference" scores, one for each response.

3. Add up the "difference" scores.

4. Divide the total of the "difference" scores by 5. The result is your discrimination score.

Pre-test Discrimination Scoresheet

RESPONSE	MY RATING	EXPERT RATING	DIFFERENCE
a	_____	– 3.0	= _____
b	_____	– 1.0	= _____
c	_____	– 5.0	= _____
d	_____	– 2.0	= _____
e	_____	– 4.0	= _____
		TOTAL	= _____
	My Discrmination Score (**TOTAL ÷ 5**)		= _____

A .5 discrmination score is considered a good score. When you have completed reading *The Art of Helping* and completed this workbook, your discrimination score will deviate one-half-level (.5) from the expert's ratings.

If you wish to check your ratings against the expert ratings here is a simple explanation. You will understand these ratings more fully after you have completed reading *The Art of Helping* text and finished the exercises in this workbook.

RESPONSE	RATING	REASON
a.	3.0	It communicates an accurate understanding of where the helpee is in terms of content and feelings expressed.
b.	1.0	It is not related to what the helpee said.
c.	5.0	It communicates an accurate understanding of where the helpee is, where she wants to be, and gives direction as to how she can get there. This response provides both understanding and direction.
d.	2.0	It is directly related to the content of the helpee's expression, but does not respond to feelings.
e.	4.0	It is an accurate response to both where the helpee is and where she wants to be.

POST-TEST DISCRIMINATION SCORESHEET

To calculate your discrimination score, use the chart below and follow these steps:

1. Fill in your ratings for each of the five responses. These ratings indicate your ratings of the effectiveness of the five responses.

2. Without regard to whether the difference is positive or negative, write the difference between your ratings and the expert ratings. This will result in five "difference" scores, one for each response.

3. Add up the "difference" scores.

4. Divide the total of the "difference" scores by 5. The result is your discrimination score.

Post-test Discrimination Scoresheet

RESPONSE	MY RATING		EXPERT RATING		DIFFERENCE
a	_____	–	2.0	=	_____
b	_____	–	4.0	=	_____
c	_____	–	1.0	=	_____
d	_____	–	5.0	=	_____
e	_____	–	3.0	=	_____
			TOTAL	=	_____
	My Discrminiation Score (**TOTAL ÷ 5**)			=	_____

(A .5 discrimination score is considered a good score.)

Check your discrimination ratings against the expert ratings.

RESPONSE	RATING	REASON
a.	2.0	It is directly related to the content of the helpee's expression; responds to content, but does not respond to feelings.
b.	4.0	It is an accurate response to both where the helpee is and where the helpee wants to be; responds to feeling and personalizes the experience.
c.	1.0	It is unrelated to the helpee's expression.
d.	5.0	It communicates an accurate understanding of where the helpee is, where the helpee wants to be, and gives direction as to how the helpee can get there. This response provides both understanding and gives direction (responds, personalizes, and initiates to facilitate action).
e.	3.0	It communicates an accurate understanding of where the helpee is in terms of content and feelings expressed; responds to feeling and content.

RATING COMMUNICATION PRE-TESTS AND POST-TESTS

Instructions

You may use the following scale to help you rate your own communication pre-test and post-test.

LEVELS OF HELPING

5.0	Initiating steps	—	Accurate response to personalized problem and goal and operational statement of steps
4.5	Defining goals	—	Accurate response to personalized problem and goal and operational definition of goal
4.0	Personalizing problem, feeling and goal	—	Accurate response to personalized problem, feeling, and goal
3.5	Personalized meaning	—	Accurate response to feeling and personalized meaning
3.0	Responding to meaning	—	Accurate response to feeling and meaning
2.5	Responding to feeling	—	Accurate response to feeling but content absent or inaccurate
2.0	Responding to content	—	Accurate response to content but feeling absent or inaccurate (e.g., accurate summary of content and/or directional advice)
1.5	Attending	—	Indirect but accurate response to content but without any direction (e.g., a relevant question, explanation of related information)
1.0	Nonattending	—	Feeling and content both absent or inaccurate

RESPONDING TO MY POST-TEST SCORES

Instructions

Assess your current interpersonal skills level by completing the following.

My pre-test communication score (page 5): _____

My post-test communication score (page 212): _____

Compare the two communication scores and respond to your experience of how you have changed in your ability to make effective responses.

I feel _____ because I _____

_____

_____

My pre-training discrimination score (page 214): _____

My post-training discrimination score (page 216): _____

Compare the two discrimination scores and respond to your experience of how you have changed in your ability to recognize effective helping responses.

I feel _____ because I _____

_____

_____

If you are dissatisfied with your post-test results, you might continue responding to yourself and develop a program to remedy the situation. Use Exercise 69 as a guide.

If you are generally satisfied with your post-test results, you might choose to continue responding to yourself and to develop a program to maximize your future learnings as you apply your "helping skills." You may also use Exercise 69 as a guide.

ANSWERS TO SELECTED EXERCISES

EXERCISE 5: DISCRIMINATING INVOLVING

1. WHO   The speaker
   WHAT   To talk
   WHEN   Monday — vague time
   WHERE   The speaker's house
   WHY   No reason given
   HOW   No specific directions given

2. WHO   The speaker
   WHAT   Work assignment
   WHEN   Not given
   WHERE   The speaker's office
   WHY   To explain reasoning — this is the speaker's purpose
   HOW   By speaker signing release slip — somewhat vague

3. WHO   The lab
   WHAT   Redo tests
   WHEN   This afternoon
   WHERE   Stay in room
   WHY   No purpose given
   HOW   Lab will pick up person

EXERCISE 8: DISCRIMINATING SELF-PREPARATION SKILLS

1. REVIEW   None
   GOAL   None
   RELAX   None

2. REVIEW   Looked at test scores and attendance
   GOAL   None
   RELAX   Closed eyes, let mind clear

3. REVIEW   Reviewed past month's behavior
   GOAL   Tell her what he had noticed and listen
   RELAX   Mental image of trout stream

EXERCISE 10: ELIMINATING DISTRACTIONS

Student could list any of the following:

1. Telephone
2. Smoking
3. Radio
4. Television
5. Foot tapping
6. Note taking
7. Outside noise
8. Interruptions
9. Excessive heat
10. Gum chewing
11. Eating
12. Excessive coughing
13. Clutter
14. Glaring lights
15. Other people talking

EXERCISE 12: DISCRIMINATING DATA FROM INFERENCES

1.	Inference		11.	Inference
2.	Inference		12.	Data
3.	Data		13.	Data
4.	Inference		14.	Data
5.	Data		15.	Inference
6.	Data		16.	Inference
7.	Inference		17.	Inference
8.	Inference		18.	Inference
9.	Data		19.	Data
10.	Inference		20.	Inference

EXERCISE 13: DRAWING INFERENCES FROM OBSERVATIONS

1. a, c, e
2. b, d, f
3. a, c, g
4. f
5. a, c
6. a, e
7. b, f
8. b
9. b, d, f
10. b, f

EXERCISE 15: PRACTICING LISTENING SKILLS

1. WHO — The speaker and others
   WHAT — Smoked grass, drank wine
   WHEN — Not stated
   WHERE — Not stated
   WHY — To have a good time, won't quit
   HOW — Not stated

2. WHO — The speaker
   WHAT — School, odd jobs
   WHEN — Past five years
   WHERE — Not stated
   WHY — Keeps quitting, doesn't know what would be better
   HOW — Not stated

3. WHO — The speaker
   WHAT — Scared of own toothache
   WHEN — Now
   WHERE — Not stated
   WHY — Pain of dental work; friend's root canal required hospitalization
   HOW — Not stated

4. WHO — The speaker
   WHAT — ADC payments
   WHEN — Now
   WHERE — Not stated
   WHY — Payments won't meet cost of raising kids
   HOW — Scrimp and save but still not enough money

5. WHO — The guard
   WHAT — Keeps nagging
   WHEN — Late night shift
   WHERE — Not stated
   WHY — "Ain't done nothing," peaceful
   HOW — Going to "kill the bastard"

EXERCISE 18: DISCRIMINATING SPECIFIC RESPONSES

1. Vague
2. Specific
3. Specific
4. Specific
5. Vague
6. Vague

EXERCISE 19: DISCRIMINATING PARAPHRASING vs. PARROTING

1.
   a. Parrot
   b. Paraphrase
   c. Paraphrase

2.
   a. Paraphrase
   b. Parrot
   c. Paraphrase

EXERCISE 20: DISCRIMINATING BRIEF RESPONSES

1. Brief and Specific
2. Brief and Specific
3. Too long
4. Too long
5. Brief and Specific

EXERCISE 21: DISCRIMINATING NONJUDGMENTAL RESPONSES

1. Nonjudgmental
2. Judgmental
3. Nonjudgmental
4. Judgmental

EXERCISE 22: DISCRIMINATING GOOD CONTENT RESPONSES

1. Poor; parrots
2. Poor; too vague
3. Good; specific, brief, and nonjudgmental
4. Poor; too long
5. Good; specific, brief, and nonjudgmental

EXERCISE 24: DISCRIMINATING ACCURATE FEELING RESPONSES

1.	a.	+	2.	a.	+	3.	a.	+
	b.	+		b.	-		b.	+
	c.	-		c.	+		c.	-

EXERCISE 25: CHOOSING ACCURATE FEELING WORDS

1. a, c, d, e, i

2. b, d, e, h, i

3. a, e, f, h

4. a, c, e, g, i

5. a, c, e, g

EXERCISE 31: DISCRIMINATING INTERCHANGEABLE RESPONSES

1. a. Wrong feeling word intensity
   b. Content not interchangeable; judgmental
   c. Good response
   d. Wrong feeling word category
   e. Content is vague

2. a. Content is vague
   b. No feeling word
   c. Parrots the response
   d. Response is too long
   e. Good response

EXERCISE 39: DISCRIMINATING PERSONALIZED MEANING

1.	a.	PM	3.	a.	IR
	b.	IR		b.	PM
	c.	PM		c.	IR
2.	a.	PM	4.	a.	PM
	b.	IR		b.	IR
	c.	PM		c.	PM

EXERCISE 41: DISCRIMINATING PERSONALIZED PROBLEM RESPONSES

1. a. PP
   b. IR
   c. PM

2. a. IR
   b. PM
   c. PP

3. a. PM
   b. IR
   c. PP

4. a. PP
   b. IR
   c. PM

EXERCISE 43: DISCRIMINATING PERSONALIZED GOAL BEHAVIOR

1. a. New Behavior
   b. Flip-side
   c. New Behavior

2. a. Flip-side
   b. Flip-side
   c. New Behavior

3. a. New Behavior
   b. Flip-side
   c. New Behavior

   a. Flip-side
   b. New Behavior
   c. Flip-side

EXERCISE 44: DISCRIMINATING PERSONALIZED GOALS

1. a. IR
   b. IR
   c. PM
   d. PP
   e. PG

2. a. PM
   b. PM
   c. PP
   d. IR
   e. PG

3. a. PP
   b. PG
   c. PM
   d. PP
   e. IR

4. a. IR
   b. PM
   c. PP
   d. PG
   e. PP

EXERCISE 52: DISCRIMINATING HELPEE BEHAVIORS IN OPERATIONALIZED GOALS

1.   a.   Helpee Behavior
        b.   Helpee Behavior
        c.   Not a Helpee Behavior

2.   a.   Not a Helpee Behavior
        b.   Helpee Behavior
        c.   Helpee Behavior

3.   a.   Helpee Behavior
        b.   Not a Helpee Behavior
        c.   Helpee Behavior

EXERCISE 53: DISCRIMINATING MEASURABLE GOALS

Students should circle the following choices in Exercise 52:

1. a & b   2. c.   3. a

EXERCISE 55: MAKING SURE THE STEPS TO A GOAL ARE BEHAVIORS

1.	Yes	6.	Yes	11.	No	16.	No	21.	Yes
2.	Yes	7.	Yes	12.	Yes	17.	No	22.	No
3.	No	8.	Yes	13.	No	18.	Yes	23.	Yes
4.	No	9.	Yes	14.	Yes	19.	No	24.	No
5.	No	10.	No	15.	No	20.	No	25.	Yes

EXERCISE 59: DISCRIMINATING TYPES OF REINFORCEMENTS

1.   a. Positive
       b. Negative
       c. Negative
       d. Positive

2.   a. Negative
       b. Negative
       c. Positive
       d. Negative

3.   a. Positive
       b. Negative
       c. Positive
       d. Negative

4.   a. Negative
       b. Positive
       c. Negative
       d. Negative

5.   a. Positive
       b. Negative
       c. Negative
       d. Negative